T0271414

Capitalism Reassessed

Capitalism Reassessed provides a broad view of different types of advanced capitalist economic systems. It is based on an empirical analysis of twenty-one OECD nations. The book looks at the reasons capitalism developed in Western Europe rather than elsewhere and shows the ways in which cultural systems closely influence economic systems. The analysis compares the economic and social performance of different capitalist economic systems along a variety of economic and social criteria. It also analyzes how capitalism will change in the twenty-first century. The appendices referred to in the book may be found at: www.swarthmore.edu/SocSci/Economics/fpryor1.

FREDERIC L. PRYOR received his Ph.D. in economics from Yale University. Although his base for more than thirty-five years has been Swarthmore College in Pennsylvania, he has also taught or carried out research at the University of Michigan, the University of California at Berkeley, the University of Indiana, Yale University, and several universities in Switzerland and France. His academic writings include twelve books in the field of economic systems and more than 120 articles in professional journals.

As a consultant, Professor Pryor has held a variety of positions, including at the World Bank, the State of Pennsylvania, the Danish government, several departments of the U.S. government, the Soros International Economic Advisory Group, the Hoover Institution, the Brookings Institution, and the Wissenschaftzentrum Berlin.

At present, he is Senior Research Scholar at Swarthmore College. He also serves on the boards of several nonprofit institutions.

Other Books by the Author

The Communist Foreign Trade System (1963)

Public Expenditures in Communist and Capitalist Nations (1968)

Property and Industrial Organization in Communist and Capitalist Nations (1973)

The Origins of the Economy: A Comparative Study of Distribution in Primitive and Peasant Economies (1977)

A Guidebook to the Comparative Study of Economic Systems (1985)

Revolutionary Grenada: A Study in Political Economy (1986)

The Political Economy of Poverty, Equity, and Growth: Malawi and Madagascar (1990)

The Red and the Green: The Rise and Fall of Collective Agriculture in Marxist Regimes (1992)

Economic Evolution and Structure: The Impact of Complexity on the U.S. Economic System (1996)

Who's Not Working and Why? Employment, Cognitive Skills, Wages and the Changing U.S. Labor Market, with David L. Schaffer (1999)

The Future of U.S. Capitalism (2002)

Economic Systems of Foraging, Agricultural, and Industrial Societies (2005)

Capitalism Reassessed

— ❖ —

Frederic L. Pryor
Swarthmore College

CAMBRIDGE
UNIVERSITY PRESS

CAMBRIDGE
UNIVERSITY PRESS

Shaftesbury Road, Cambridge CB2 8EA, United Kingdom

One Liberty Plaza, 20th Floor, New York, NY 10006, USA

477 Williamstown Road, Port Melbourne, VIC 3207, Australia

314–321, 3rd Floor, Plot 3, Splendor Forum, Jasola District Centre, New Delhi – 110025, India

103 Penang Road, #05–06/07, Visioncrest Commercial, Singapore 238467

Cambridge University Press is part of Cambridge University Press & Assessment, a department of the University of Cambridge.

We share the University's mission to contribute to society through the pursuit of education, learning and research at the highest international levels of excellence.

www.cambridge.org
Information on this title: www.cambridge.org/9780521190206

First published 2010
First paperback edition 2013

A catalogue record for this publication is available from the British Library

Library of Congress Cataloging-in-Publication data
Pryor, Frederic L.
    Capitalism reassessed / Frederic L. Pryor.
        p.   cm.
    Includes bibliographical references and index.
    ISBN 978-0-521-19020-6 (hardback)
    1. Capitalism – Case studies.   2. Capitalism – Cross cultural studies.
    I. Title.
    HB501.P78 2010
    330.12′2–dc22   2010021142

ISBN   978-0-521-19020-6   Hardback
ISBN   978-1-107-61635-6   Paperback

Additional resources for this publication at
www.swarthmore.edu/SocSci/Economics/fpryor1

To the memory of Zora

Contents

List of Tables and Figures   *page* ix

Acknowledgments   xi

1 Introduction   1

2 What Is Capitalism?   6

3 Origins of Capitalism   20

4 Varieties of Capitalism in Industrialized Nations   74

5 Cultural Influences on the Economic System   112

6 Do Some Economic Systems Perform Better Than Others?   146

Contents

7 Happiness and Economic Systems   184

8 How Capitalism Will Change   205

Bibliography   247

Index   265

Tables and Figures

Tables

3–1 The Thresholds of Capitalism, Per Capita
GDP, and Urbanization   *page* 24

3–2 Average Long-Term Nominal Commercial
Interest Rates for Selected Countries in the
Seventeenth and Eighteenth Centuries   46

3–3 Adult Literacy Rates in the Nineteenth
Century   50

4–1 The Derived Economic Systems in the
OECD Nations in 1990   86

4–2 Defining Characteristics of the Four
Industrial Capitalist Economic Systems
in 1990   90

5–1 Cultural and Economic Systems of OECD
Nations in 1990   116

5–2 Indicators Used to Derive the Cultural
Systems   118

Tables and Figures

6–1 Future Development of Countries with
Positive Political Freedom and Low Capitalism
Scores in the Nineteenth Century   150
6–2 Cultural, Economic, and Performance
Systems of the OECD Nations around 1990   158
6–3 OECD Outcome Statistics   164
7–1 Basic Data on Happiness for the 1990s 191
7–2 Estimates Showing the Determinants
of the Level of Happiness   196
8–1 GDP Growth and Fluctuations in Industrial
Capitalist Nations, 1975–2007   207

Figures

4–1 Designation of Clusters   77
6–1 Two Types of Causation   153

Acknowledgments

In the past decade I have written a series of technical articles for professional journals on particular aspects of capitalism. This book reports many of my results, but it is written without economic jargon and in readable English, with technical matters placed in the appendices, so that my arguments and evidence are accessible to a broad audience. I am grateful for the suggestions to improve the manuscript from Robert DuPlessis, Edward Fuller, Joseph Gormally, Lillian Li, Dan Pryor, Victoria Wilson-Schwartz, and some anonymous referees, as well as Zora Pryor and the scores of colleagues who provided useful assistance for improving the various essays on which this book is based. None should be blamed, however, for my errors.

Capitalism Reassessed

— ✤ CHAPTER ONE ✤ —

Introduction

The economic crisis that almost all industrial capitalist nations experienced at the end of the first decade of the twenty-first century has given rise to questions about the nature of capitalism that are seldom asked when times are good: What is capitalism? How does it usually perform? Where are we going? Do we need to totally change our economic system to avoid another economic meltdown in the future?

When I converse with others about our economic system, I often feel we are talking past each other. They seem to consider only one arrangement of institutions and policies as "capitalism" and everything else as some other economic system, such as "socialism" or "fascism." On the contrary, I believe that capitalist economic systems appear in many forms and that a broader view is important, an approach necessary so that trade-offs before us regarding institutions and policies can be more clearly evaluated. Although we live in a capitalist economy system, it is often difficult to gain a perspective on how its important institutions work together as a system.

The purpose of this short book, aimed at a general audience, is to provide a broad view of the economics of capitalism – its origins, the different ways in which its institutions can be structured, its performance in recent years, and the directions of its institutional development in the coming years. I carry out the discussion by defining, comparing, and contrasting four different types of capitalist economic systems. I then show that these groupings of capitalist systems parallel the four types of pattern of cultural values of the population. These four economic systems differ significantly, however, in their economic and social performance. Nevertheless, the countries with economic systems that score higher for one set of performance indicators tend to score lower than countries with other economic systems for a different set of indicators, so that there appears to be a trade-off. Nevertheless, we could not find any evidence that any of these economic systems produced happier people.

This institutional approach means, however, that I neglect particular policies by the governments (or by industries) that vary among countries with the same set of institutions. And, in order to focus on more narrowly economic issues, I leave it to others to make moral judgments about various institutions and other aspects of capitalism.

This book differs from many other recent studies on capitalism in that it contains an empirical analysis of the similarities and differences between various types of capitalist economies, and the impact of these organizational arrangements on the performance of their economies. Many other books on the economic systems are highly abstract, so that it is difficult to apply their descriptions to the real world around us. Still others are highly ideological, drawing arguments from selected anecdotes that suit the author's economic or political predilections. Finally, others focus primarily on a single country and, with a bit of hand-waving, proclaim other capitalist countries to be "similar." In contrast, I have tried to keep the discussion as concrete as possible, drawing empirical evidence from the experience of the twenty-one industrial nations that belong to the Organisation for Economic Co-operation and Development (OECD).

Such a comparative approach allows us to see the similarities and differences between the various capitalist nations under consideration. Moreover, I have also taken pains to avoid most ideological arguments, although I do test several against actual data, for instance, to determine whether people in countries with particular capitalist systems are happier than those living in other capitalist systems.

The reassessment of capitalism in this book does not provide solutions to our present economic difficulties, since its focus is primarily on the structure of the economy and its institutions. It does, however, provide a point of view about the essential aspects of the system so that the implications of proposed institutional changes can be evaluated in a broader context than the immediate problems at hand.

The discussion in the following pages takes a straightforward route. The next chapter is a short clarification of what "capitalism" means, and it is then followed in Chapter 3 by an exploration of the historical origins of capitalism. In Chapter 4 I look at the institutional configuration of industrialized OECD nations and distinguish four different types of capitalist economic systems. In the following Chapter 5, I examine the particular types of cultural values that influence how these four economic systems are structured. Chapter 6 analyzes the performance of the four different types of capitalist systems in recent years, as measured by a variety of economic and social indicators. Chapter 7 briefly explores whether the degree of happiness in these nations, as reported in various public opinion polls, is related to the economic system. The book ends with a discussion of how capitalism is changing and what possibilities lie ahead for it.

Introduction

Of course, there are many issues concerning capitalism that I do not discuss in this short book, for instance,
capitalist ideology, changes in capitalist institutions over
the last few centuries, or many social and moral aspects
of capitalism, such as what this economic system does to
people's characters.

Nevertheless, I try to provide new insights into the
nature of capitalism so that we have a compass with
which to steer our economic system in a direction to
avoid the shoals of fruitless debate about our institutions
that have marred our efforts to solve our present economic difficulties.

— ❖ CHAPTER TWO ❖ —

What Is Capitalism?

Capitalism is a protean concept with a variety of definitions. To avoid confusion and to allow for a straightforward analysis, it is first necessary to define my subject matter. I bear in mind, however, a serious warning: "The surest way to fail as an author is to start by sounding pedantic, and the surest way to sound pedantic is to start with an unexhilarating search for definitions."[1] I plead guilty.

This chapter starts with general definitions of the terms "economic system" and "capitalism." I then explore some of the important implications of the definition of capitalism to specify the dimensions along which it can be quantified, so that in later chapters I can quantify the degree of capitalism in each of about ninety nations. The

---

[1] Carlo Cipolla, *Literacy and Development in the West* (Baltimore, MD: Penguin Books, 1969), 11.

footnotes present references and additional explanations, while the technical appendices to the book appear on my Web site.[2]

A. Definitions and Some Implications

1. Some Definitions

The word "capitalism" began to appear in various Western languages less than three centuries ago (see Appendix 2–1 for a discussion of its etymology), and over the succeeding centuries the concept has acquired various meanings. Some writers have used the term "capitalism" simply to designate ordinary trade in which credit and financial instruments play a large role, which is carried out in order to accumulate more wealth (commercial capitalism), an approach also followed in a broader manner by many of the classical economists. Others have placed primary emphasis on the presence of institutions of private property and enforcement of contract. Still others have linked capitalism to particular methods of industrial production involving hired labor or to special attitudes toward commercial activities (the "spirit of capitalism"). Marxist-oriented commentators

---

[2] http://www.swarthmore.edu/SocSci/Economics/fpryor1/. The third link on this Web page leads to the appendices to this book.

define capitalism as a "mode of production" in which the market dominates distribution; ownership of the means of production is private; labor does not receive the full value of its output; and wealth is concentrated in ever-fewer hands. In contrast, liberal economists focus primarily on free individual producers selling goods and services and consumers buying them in a market economy.

Let's start at the beginning. An economic system is usually defined in a very general manner, for instance, as the totality of institutions and organizations that specify property relations and have an important influence in channeling the production and distribution of goods and services. The economic policies or performance arising from decisions made by the functionaries of these institutions and organizations are *not* included in the definition of the system; instead, they are viewed as a result of it. Such an abstract approach is, of course, far removed from the world around us, but it allows us to define specific economic systems in many different ways.

In general, capitalism is an economic system in which goods, labor, land, and financial services are transferred through relatively competitive markets and in which the means of production are primarily owned privately or by groups of individuals, rather than by governments. A "relatively competitive market" is one in which most prices fluctuate according to the strength of supply and demand forces; most markets are not dominated by monopolies or guilds regulating the entry of new producers into the market or the prices at which goods and services are sold; and government regulations and other policies do not play a commanding role in the actions of the market but act to protect property and enforce contracts.

This very broad definition, however, tells us nothing about government-fixed prices and wages, pervasive technical regulations and standards, oligopolistic or monopolistic markets, or the variety of ways in which an actual economic system allocates goods and services. Nevertheless, it does have one critical advantage: it implies that there are degrees to which an economic system can be considered capitalist.[3] Let us consider that on one end of the spectrum is an economy in which all goods and services are allocated in perfectly competitive markets, with just enough government regulation for the system to maintain itself and not self-destruct. Then we can set

---

[3] Some believe that, just as a woman cannot be "a little bit pregnant," an economy cannot have lower or higher degrees of capitalism. Underlying this belief is the false assumption that all the institutions that make up a capitalist economy are unchangeable once they reach a particular level and, moreover, that this level is reached at the same time for all of the criteria used to define capitalism.

up scales rating the degree to which economic systems approach this standard; we can also define cut-off points at which to exclude from the capitalist camp economies that do not meet certain minimum criteria, even though they may have some capitalistic elements. Such an approach departs from the practice of some political conservatives of defining capitalism in terms of a strict laissez-faire government and perfect competition.

In Chapter 4, I show that in various capitalist economies different institutions can carry out particular economic functions; for instance, pensions can be distributed through insurance funds or through a government fund. And such institutions can distinguish different types of capitalist economies. Moreover, as I argue in Chapter 8, the financial institutions of an economic system are critically important in capitalism. To make this general definition more precise so that the degree of capitalism can be measured, it is important to consider several measurable elements of capitalism, namely, the level of economic development, the conditions facing the producers of goods and services, and the conditions facing consumers.

a. Level of Economic Development. At all levels of economic development almost all economies, including foraging and primitive agricultural societies have had markets of one type or another.[4] We read, for instance, of the great trading empires of the Phoenicians or Greeks. For the most part, however, in economies with low levels of economic development, only a small share of goods and services, labor, land, and finance passed through these markets. Although farmers in an agricultural society may sell 10 percent of their crops to the city in order to purchase factory goods, it is not meaningful to label such an economic system as capitalist. Capitalism should be considered to be present only when the economic development of a nation is high enough to make a large tradable surplus available for such market activities.[5]

So where does one draw the line? For the nineteenth century, it is useful to start with the estimations of Irma Adelman and Cynthia Taft Morris,[6] who tried to assess

---

[4] Frederic L. Pryor, *The Origins of the Economy: A Comparative Study of Distribution in Primitive and Peasant Economies* (New York: Academic Press, 1977).

[5] A number of nineteenth-century social scientists who proposed stage theories of economic development placed capitalism at the top. They did not realize that communist economies, with or without central planning, can also have large tradable surpluses.

[6] Irma Adelman and Cynthia Taft Morris, "Patterns of Market Expansion in the Nineteenth Century: A Quantitative Study," pp. 231–325 in George Dalton, ed., *Research in Economic Anthropology*, vol. 1 (Greenwich, CT: JAI Press, 1978). One can, of course, niggle with some of the Adelman-Morris results, for instance, that

the extent to which goods, labor services, land, and finance in a particular country are purchased through markets. For each country, I have selected a cut-off point for defining its economy as capitalist as the year in which the average of the transactions in these markets reaches 50 percent of the total goods, labor services, land, and finance. For Great Britain, this would be 1816, when, as almost all historians agree, the country had a capitalist economic system. Unfortunately, the Adelman-Morris data do not extend into the twentieth century, but since per capita gross domestic product (GDP, the total amount of produced goods and services) is highly correlated with the Adelman-Morris estimates of marketization, this measure can serve as a useful proxy to broaden the sample.[7] In 1816 Great Britain had a per capita GDP of $1,689 in the purchasing power of 1990 dollars. I therefore use this as the lowest level of economic development a nation in the twentieth century must have to

England passed the 50 percent marketization level before the Netherlands. But small changes in their estimates do not change the general results that I obtain using their estimates.

[7] Readers should be warned, however, that it is not a perfect proxy. For instance, in 1816 only one other country, the Netherlands, had a higher per capita GDP than Great Britain, but in that year the Netherlands did not appear to meet the marketable surplus criterion discussed earlier.

warrant investigation of its other elements of capitalism.[8] Countries with per capita GDPs lower than this amount may contain "islands of capitalism," but the entire economy cannot be characterized as capitalist.

b. Conditions Facing Producers of Goods and Services. In capitalism private ownership of the means of production must predominate, and producers must have a certain amount of security for their property. This means that property cannot be expropriated by the government or by other private individuals except under very special circumstances, such as for the repayment of overdue debts. Moreover, producers' contracts with customers and suppliers must be enforceable, which requires independent and honest dispute-resolution mechanisms, such as courts. Chapter 4 shows how these conditions can be measured. Moreover, to survive in the marketplace, producers must strive to maximize profits by, for instance, improving their products; introducing new products and production methods; buying their inputs at the lowest possible price; setting their prices to maximize the difference between their costs and their revenues;

---

[8] Angus Maddison, *The World Economy: Historical Statistics* (Paris: OECD, 2003). More technically, Maddison's GDP estimates are calculated in 1990 international Geary-Khamis dollars.

and accumulating more capital to increase their productivity. The existence of these conditions can also be measured.

c. Conditions Facing Consumers. In a capitalist system, consumers must be able to purchase the goods and services they desire if they have the money (or credit) to pay for them. Although all countries restrict the purchase of certain goods and services (for instance, illegal drugs or pornography), in capitalist countries such restrictions are relatively minor. The extent of such restrictions can also be measured.

What role does the government play in a capitalist system? There is no simple answer to this question. Aside from providing some of the conditions producers and consumers need, governments must at least supply such public goods as roads and police protection, because it is unlikely that these would be supplied privately or, if they were, in a manner that encourages production and trade. Courts, education, and similar services are also needed. These, too, can be supplied privately, but they are usually most efficiently financed or supplied by the government.

There are certain things that in capitalism a government must refrain from doing. It cannot ban certain forms of productive organizations, such as corporations, which allow large-scale capital accumulation. Moreover, it cannot directly control most production, set most prices, or determine to a significant extent what is to be produced or distributed. The government can, however, exercise indirect influences on producers by, for instance, setting health and safety standards, banning production of certain products considered harmful, or enforcing antitrust regulations. In brief, as Adam Smith noted several centuries ago, capitalism does not imply complete laissez faire.

In the late 1990s the OECD nations that are studied in further chapters all met this market/income criterion of capitalism. Moreover, all have predominantly private ownership of the means of production; all have relatively free competition (especially as the importance of foreign trade increases and trade barriers are low), and all have relatively few restrictions on consumers.[9]

---

[9] Data on public ownership and industrial concentration for OECD countries in the 1960s can be found in Frederic L. Pryor, "The Extent and Pattern of Public Ownership in Developed Economies," *Weltwirtschaftliches Archiv* 102, no. 1 (1970): 159–88; and "An International Comparison of Concentration Ratios," *Review of Economics and Statistics* 54, no. 2 (May 1972): 130–40. Most (but not all) met the various criteria for capitalism at that time. Since then, most have denationalized industries and, moreover, their market competition has increased due to lower trade barriers and greater foreign trade.

2. What Capitalism Is Not

It is often claimed that capitalism cannot be analyzed strictly in economic terms and that certain key political and social characteristics must be brought into the discussion. This assertion is overdrawn.

Many people argue that there is an intimate association between capitalism and democracy. Chapter 4 shows that, although the degrees of capitalism and democracy are highly correlated today, this does not indicate a causal relationship in either direction. Democracy does not inevitably give rise to capitalism, nor does capitalism inevitably lead to democracy. I also show that changes in the degrees of capitalism and democracy are not correlated over time.

A Marxist approach toward the analysis of capitalism emphasizes the presence of at least two social classes: the owners of the means of production, who receive the profits earned from their property and use such profits to accumulate more capital, and those working for them, who sell their labor on a market, do not receive as wages the full value of what they produce (and are, therefore, exploited), and do not have control over their work. Emphasizing these characteristics omits the fact that many of these conditions are not unique to capitalism; they are, rather, the features of modern industrial production. For instance, in the centrally planned communist countries of Eastern Europe during the second half of the twentieth century, the workers also did not receive wages reflecting the full value of what they produced; they usually did not have control over their work; and they did not own the means of production in any real sense. Moreover, in these economies, an elite managed the factories, made the key economic and political decisions (usually with little consultation with the workers), and received higher salaries.

Beginning with the writings of Max Weber and his followers,[10] many economists have also argued that capitalism involves a certain set of values, a "market mentality" that drives its possessors to accumulate capital and become rich. The relationship between capitalism and values is not, however, straightforward. Although a market-driven economy implies a certain individualism, group identities can still be strong. While attitudes toward market activities and other ways to achieve renown are certainly important,[11] other important attitudes and values can be quite different. These issues are discussed in detail in Chapter 5. At this point, however, it is worth

[10] Max Weber, *The Protestant Ethic and the Spirit of Capitalism*, trans. Talcott Parsons. (New York: Routledge, 1930 [1905]).

[11] This is particularly emphasized by Albert O. Hirschman, *The Passions and the Interests: Political Arguments for Capitalism before Its Triumph* (Princeton, NJ: Princeton University Press, 1977).

noting that in today's world, as this chapter shows, there is little relationship between the prevailing values and the *degree* of capitalism, but there is a strong one between the *type* of capitalism and the dominant values of the population.

3. Quantitative Estimates of Capitalism

For the nineteenth century we have few quantitative measures of the economic institutions of various countries and must rely on rough estimates of the degree of marketization of goods, services, and factors of production, a calculation that is discussed in greater detail in Chapter 3 and Appendix 3–1. For the twentieth century, by contrast, we can employ a number of measures of institutions, as discussed in Appendix 2–2, to measure the degree of capitalism in each of eighty-eight nations in the year 2000. The result of such calculations can be found in Appendix Table A-6 and make a cameo appearance in Chapter 4. At this point, it is also worth noting that although the degree of capitalism is significantly correlated with the level of economic development, as measured by the per capita GDP, this variable explains somewhat less than half of the variation in the degree of capitalism in this sample of nations. Other factors, such as the type of capitalism (discussed in Chapter 4), the average level of education, and a variety of historical factors (discussed in Chapter 3), also play a causal role.

B. A Concluding Note

The preliminaries are now over. I've presented a brief, general definition of capitalism, looked at certain implications of the definition, and used some of these implications to provide a framework for measuring the degree of capitalism in a given society. Of course, definitions and quantitative scales by themselves signify little. But a judicious use of these definitions and scales allows us to gain a broader view of capitalist economic systems: how they started, how they perform, and in what direction they are changing.

— ✤ CHAPTER THREE ✤ —

Origins of Capitalism

I f we look back several centuries, we see a variety of factors that could have provided the conditions under which capitalism could arise. By taking a comparative view of countries in the "long eighteenth century" (roughly 1650–1815), we gain insight into the nature of capitalism and why it first arose in northwestern Europe instead of places such as China, India, or Japan, whose prospects for capitalism in 1700 may have appeared more promising.[1]

---

[1] Recently Eric Mielants in *The Origins of Capitalism and the Rise of the West* (Philadelphia: Temple University Press, 2007) examines why capitalism did not arise in the Middle East and northern Africa, but space constrains me to focus on China, India, and Japan. For the Middle East, see Timur Kuran, *The Long Divergence: How Islamic Law Held Back the Middle East.* (Princeton, NJ: Princeton University Press, 2010).

Origins of Capitalism

There is no single or simple explanation of how capitalism originated. Those who claim to have found one are either ignoring the variety of factors at work or proposing a "cause" that is too general to illuminate the particulars of any specific case. Moreover, an explanation that seems quite useful for understanding the development of capitalism in one country may shed little light on its development in another. In recent years, most analyses have used one or more of the following five very general arguments to explain why capitalism arose in northwestern Europe, rather than other parts of the world:

1. By 1700, the nations in northwestern Europe had a higher level of economic development, a greater stock of physical capital, and a higher level of technology than other countries, so that the transition to the new economic system was easier.

2. By the eighteenth century, northwestern Europe was developing economic institutions that were more conducive to economic development, such as security of property, contract enforcement, education of the citizenry, organizations to promote the spread of new knowledge, efficient arrangements for conducting business, and freer markets for labor and capital.

3. Over time, governments in northwestern Europe took measures that were more supportive of domestic

trade and production; aided foreign trade through colonialism; and, because of limited political powers, interfered less in market activities.

4. "Modern" values and cultural factors had taken hold in northwestern Europe more than elsewhere, and these were more favorable to capitalism.

5. Environmental factors were more advantageous for economic development in northwest Europe than in Asia.

This chapter examines each of these five arguments. In some cases, we will find that the specified conditions contributed strongly to the origin of capitalism in northwest Europe; in other cases, their role was quite unimportant; and in still others, no definite conclusion can be drawn. As noted below, of the five arguments, several still seem relevant for explaining the current trajectory of capitalism in industrial nations.

A single chapter, of course, cannot provide a detailed explanation of how capitalism began in any specific country. To apply the five arguments discussed above in a rigorous way, we would need to canvas all a nation's particularities, a task that must be left to specialized monographs. This survey, in brief, is like a photograph taken from outer space, not a detailed map, of the origins of capitalism in different parts of the world.

A. The Influence of the Level of Economic Development

As explained in the previous chapter, there are different degrees of capitalism, but I date the point at which a nation steps over the threshold into an early stage of capitalism in the year when an average of half the goods, labor, land, and finance in a nation are transferred through a market. This estimation provides us a footing to start the analysis of possible factors influencing the introduction of capitalism. Table 3–1 presents such estimates for a number of countries, along with per capita GDPs in 1820 and urbanization rates for three years in the eighteenth century.[2]

Countries with higher levels of economic development (high per capita GDPs) tended to achieve a capitalist economic system at an earlier date than other nations. More specifically, we see a positive relation between the year

[2] Appendix 3–1 discusses the calculation of the thresholds of capitalism of various countries, which are based on the degree to which the exchange of goods, labor, land, and finance pass through markets, as estimated by Irma Adelman and Cynthia Taft Morris in "Patterns of Market Expansion in the Nineteenth Century: A Quantitative Study." In George Dalton, ed. *Research in Economic Anthropology*, vol.1 (Greenwich, CT: JAI Press, 1987), 231–325

Table 3-1. The Thresholds of Capitalism, Per Capita GDP, and Urbanization

	Capitalist Threshold Year	Per Capita GDP, 1820	Urbanization		
			1700	1750	1800
England	1816	$1,706	13–16%	17–19%	22–24%
Belgium	1829	1,319	26–35	18–23	18–22
USA	1832	1,257	n.a.	n.a.	5.3[a]
Netherlands	1833	1,838	38–49	33–41	34–39
France	1838	1,135	11–15	12–16	11–13
Switzerland	1847	1,090	6–8	6–9	6–8
Germany	1855	1,077	8–11	8–10	8–10
Austria	1855	1,218	5–8[b]	6–7[b]	6–7[b]
Sweden	1864	1,198	5–8[c]	6–9[c]	8–10[c]
Denmark	1869	1,274	5–8[c]	6–9[c]	8–10[c]
Canada	1875	904	n.a.	n.a.	5.3[a]
Australia	1875	518	n.a.	n.a.	n.a.
Italy	1878	1,117	14–19	15–20	16–20
Spain	1881	1,008	12–17	12–18	12–19
New Zealand	1884	400	n.a.	n.a.	n.a.
Norway	1886	1,104	5–8[c]	6–9[c]	8–10[c]

Japan	1893	669	11–14	n.a.	14.5
Mexico	1894	759	n.a.	n.a.	n.a.
Greece	1897	641	n.a.	n.a.	n.a.
Portugal	>1900	923	18–23	13–15	14–17
Russia	>1900	689	4–7	5–7	5–7
Balkans	>1900	682[e]	7–12[d]	7–12[d]	8–11[d]
China	>1900	600	n.a.	n.a.	6–7.5[e]

Notes: The determination of the capitalist threshold year is discussed in Chapter 2. The per capita GDP data are in 1990 dollars. Urbanization is defined as the ratio of population in towns 5,000 and over to the total population.

n.a. = not available.

a = U.S. + Canada

b = Austria-Hungary

c = Scandinavia (weighted average for Denmark, Norway, and Sweden)

d = weighted average for Albania and former Yugoslavia, in 1870

e = in 1840

Urbanization data come from Paul Bairoch, *Cities and Economic Development from the Dawn of History to the Present* (Chicago: University of Chicago Press. 1988), pp. 215, 290, 356, 360, and 430. For Japan, Thomas C. Smith, *The Agrarian Origins of Modern Japan* (Stanford, CA: Stanford University Press, 1959), 68, reports an estimate for 1750 of 22 percent. The per capita GDP data come from Angus Maddison, *The World Economy: Historical Statistics* (Paris: OECD, 2003).

a country reached the capitalist threshold in the nineteenth century and its per capita GDP in 1820.[3] But it must also be noted that some countries with relatively high per capita income levels did *not* have a capitalist economic system according to my definition, so my generalization about the relation of capitalism to a relatively high per capita GDP must be considered as a probability statement and not an absolute law. For instance, a conspicuous European exception to the generalization is the Netherlands. Its per capita GDP was the highest in the world in the eighteenth century, but before it reached the capitalist threshold, according to my marketization criterion, its level of development fell 14 percent between 1700 and 1820. According to these estimates, the Netherlands did not actually reach the capitalist threshold until 1833.[4]

Did capitalism originate in northwestern Europe because it had a higher level of economic development than other regions in the world? For many years this has been considered obvious, but more recently, some economic historians have disputed this notion. It is therefore

---

[3] The coefficient of determination (R^2) = .61. This designates the degree of explanatory power of the regression and runs from 0.00 to 1.00.

[4] The data come from Angus Maddison, *The World Economy: Historical Statistics* (Paris: OECD, 2003).

necessary to look more carefully at the evidence on the level of development.

1. A Macroeconomic Indicator of Development: Per Capita Gross Domestic Product

Although per capita GDP is by no means a perfect indicator of the relative level of economic development, it is the best and most available measure that we have, and the most comparable from country to country. Macroeconomic estimates of per capita GDP throughout the world by Angus Maddison suggest that by the eighteenth century, northwestern Europe was far ahead of the rest of the world and was thus more favorably situated to develop capitalism.[5] More specifically, in 1700, western Europe had an average per capita GDP (in 1990 dollars) of $998, and the three richest nations were the Netherlands, the United Kingdom (that is, the region now so designated), and Belgium, all situated in the northwestern part of the continent. By contrast, in 1700, China, India, and Japan had per capita GDPs of $600, $669, and $550, respectively. In that year, the levels of per capita GDPs in Eastern Europe, Latin America, and the rest of Asia were roughly similar to those of China

[5] Ibid.

and India, while African developmental levels were considerably lower. Other scholars support this general conclusion with estimates of the standard of living in Europe and Asia.[6]

Although this would seem an open-and-shut case for the higher level of development in northwestern Europe, Kenneth Pomeranz has recently challenged it, arguing that in the eighteenth century, levels of economic development in northwestern Europe and Asia were roughly similar.[7] However, he bases this claim on earlier estimates of per capita GDP, which have recently come under sharp and justifiable criticism.[8] As supporting evidence, he also

[6] Robert Allen and his co-authors in "Wages, Prices, and Living Standards in China" (www.iisg.nl/hpw/papers/allen-et-al.pdf, 2005) estimate the standard of living of construction workers in Beijing, Canton, Sichuan, Kyoto-Edo, and leading cities of Europe in the eighteenth century. Their data suggest that the standard of living in these Asian cities was far below that of London and Amsterdam, but roughly equivalent to that of Milan and Leipzig. Although this indicates that the level of economic development was higher in northwestern Europe than in Asia, it focuses only on several major cities and on just one slice of the population.

[7] Kenneth Pomeranz, *The Great Divergence* (Princeton, NJ: Princeton University Press, 2000).

[8] He draws primarily on Paul Bairoch, "The Main Trends in National Economic Disparities since the Industrial Revolution." In Paul Bairoch and Maurice Levy-Leboyer, eds. *Disparities in Economic Development since the Industrial Revolution* (New York: St. Martin's

cites estimates of energy usage, which, in predominantly agricultural societies, does not necessarily reflect the overall level of economic development.[9] Finally, he also uses data on life expectancy to buttress his argument, but more recent life expectancy data also contradict his results. Until these data problems are resolved, we cannot determine the validity of conclusions drawn from his

Press, 1975), 3–17; and "Écarts internationaux des niveaux de vie avant la révolution industrielle," *Annales: Économies, Sociétés, Civilisation* 34, no. 1 (January 1979): 145–72. The critiques of these estimates have focused on Bairoch's methodology, his data, and his inconsistencies. See, for instance, Angus Maddison, "A Comparison of Levels of GDP Per Capita in Developed and Developing Countries, 1700–1980," *Journal of Economic History* 43, no. 1 (March 1983): 27–41; his "Measuring European Growth: The Core and the Periphery." In Erik Aerts and N. Valério, eds., *Proceedings of the Tenth International Economic History Congress* (Leuven, 1990); and his *The World Economy*, 248–50. It is unfortunate that Bairoch has died and his detailed explanation of these estimates is found only in a mimeographed manuscript that is not listed in the Bairoch archive www.unil.ch/ihes/page14314.html and is apparently unavailable.

[9] Pomeranz uses estimates by Vaclav Smil (*Energy in World History* [Boulder, CO: Westview, 1994], 234) that by 1700 "typical levels of energy use … were still broadly similar in China and northwestern Europe." But energy requirements for preindustrial agricultural economies depend on the soil, rainfall, motive power, and other environmental conditions and do not necessarily reflect the level of economic development.

demographic approach.[10] At the present time, however, Pomeranz's attack on the conventional belief about the higher level of economic development in northwestern Europe than in Asia does not seem convincing.

2. A Microeconomic Indicator of Development: Technology

Underlying a country's level of economic development, of course, are the technologies it employs in production, a feature of the economy providing considerable insight into the origins of capitalism. In his *Novum Organum* (1626), Francis Bacon proclaimed that the foundations of the modern life were printing, gunpowder, and the

---

[10] Pomeranz, *op. cit.*, compares scattered data on life expectancy in northwestern Europe in the seventeenth to early nineteenth centuries with similar statistics for Japan and finds that the Japanese lived at least as long as Europeans and probably longer. Although China's life expectancy numbers were not so impressive, they were also quite comparable to those of Europeans. Only India seemed to have lower life expectancies than Europe at that time. Pomeranz also claims that many cities in southeast Asia were far ahead of that in Western Europe in matters of sanitation and provision of clean water.

But such evidence has been recently challenged, and Peter Lindert's collection of life expectancy data ("Life Expectancy Data," http://gpih.ucdavis.edu/Evidence.htm) reveal a different picture. In the seventeenth and eighteenth centuries, England, Denmark, and Sweden had the highest life expectancy at birth (33–39), followed closely by Japan.

compass. All three came from China and were common there during the latter part of the Sung dynasty (969 A.D.–1279 A.D.), diffusing to Europe many centuries later. Most observers agree, therefore, that before the seventeenth century, China appears to have had a technological advantage. As early as the Han dynasty (207 B.C.–220 A.D.) in China there was widespread use of a curved moldboard iron plow. China also invented the collar harness that permitted animals to be used for plowing and developed the multitube seed drill. Moreover, Chinese artisans used coal in producing iron, made steel from cast iron, and were the first to drill for natural gas.[11] These and other technologies did not reach Europe for many centuries. Pomeranz points out other examples of superior technology that had developed in Asia by 1700, such as irrigated agriculture, canal and lock construction, and textile weaving and dyeing. Although northwestern Europe had better individual power-generating machines (water wheels), China had a marked advantage in the efficiency of its stoves for both cooking and heating. Based on technology, the development of

---

[11] Smil, *op. cit.*, p. 232. Other material in this paragraph come from Pomeranz, *op. cit.*, pp. 43–68; and Michael Mann, "European Development: Approaching a Historical Explanation." In Jean Baechler, John A. Hall, and Michael Mann, eds., *Europe and the Rise of Capitalism* (New York: Blackwell, 1988), 1–6.

capitalism appeared more likely in Asia than in Europe, at least by 1700. It must be added, however, that a great many of these Asian technologies were made before 1000 A.D., and, for unclear reasons, Asian technology did not maintain its rapid advance thereafter.

Currently, most scholars believe that technological parity between northwestern Europe and China was roughly achieved at least by the beginning of the eighteenth century and that, by the end of the century, Europe had sprinted ahead with the spate of new inventions accompanying the rise of industrialization.[12] Of course, inventions per se are not sufficient for economic advance; they must be put into use. I argue below that the institutions fostering the diffusion of technological and scientific knowledge were more effective in northwestern Europe than in Asia. More favorable European environmental conditions also played a role in some cases, as shown by the spread of the technology for producing iron. Chinese use of coal to make iron and steel

---

[12] Some scholars, such as Michael Mann, "European Development: Approaching a Historical Explanation." In Jean Baechler, et al., eds., *Europe and the Rise of Capitalism*. (New York: Blackwell, 1988), 1–6, claim that European technology began to surpass China's in the mid-fifteenth century, the period of European naval expansion, and continued in the next century (with the Galilean revolution in science).

began in the Sung dynasty (969 A.D.–1126 A.D.); but thereafter, the use of coal seemed confined primarily to several northern provinces, where it was readily available. When this technique was later developed in northwestern Europe, the greater dispersion of coal resources over the continent allowed its use over a wider area.

3. Conclusions

Despite some doubtful claims to the contrary, the available evidence strongly suggests that the level of economic development in northwestern Europe, as measured by per capita GDP, was higher than that of China, Japan, and India by 1700. Although Asian technology was not stagnant from the twelfth to eighteenth centuries, it appears that northwestern Europe had caught up by the end of the period and was surpassing the three Asian countries. Although a rising level of economic development is not a sufficient condition for capitalism, it is certainly a necessary one. Northwestern Europe was, therefore, a more likely birthplace for capitalism than the leading Asian nations.

B. The Influence of Institutional Developments

A number of institutions are necessary for capitalism to arise and flourish. There must be markets, banks, and other organizations to allow the transfer of payments for goods, services, and factors of production; a trading infrastructure; mobile workers who are not legally bound to any owners as serfs or slaves; domestic peace; and laws or institutions that effectively provide security of property and enforcement of contract.

Some well-known legal scholars trace the origins of capitalism in Europe to the institutional reforms of Pope Gregory VII (1073–1085),[13] who tried to separate the church from secular authority, and, at the same time, to centralize power within the church. To govern this newly independent church entity, these Gregorian reforms gave rise to the new canon law, which shortly thereafter served as a model for new secular legal systems, including laws establishing and governing the activities of other corporate groups, and laws controlling trade activities (*lex mercatoria*). These secular laws, it is argued, allowed the establishment of the economic institutions and practices that eventually led to capitalism.

---

[13] Most notably, Harold J. Berman in *Law and Revolution: The Formation of the Western Legal Tradition* (Cambridge, MA: Harvard University Press, 1983). Proving these linkages requires much more evidence. Moreover, some Asian nations, such as China, also appeared to have well-developed, mercantile law, according to various essays in Kathryn Bernhardt and Philip C. C. Huang, eds., *Civil Law in Qing and Republican China* (Stanford, CA: Stanford University Press, 1994).

Although this thesis is fascinating, proving such causal linkages between these historical developments lies beyond the scope of this study. The discussion below focuses on more concrete institutions and activities, namely, markets, urbanization, security of private property, contract enforcement, and education and the spread of knowledge. In most of these cases, northwestern Europe was in a more favorable position for capitalist development than Asia.

1. Markets

Market exchange of goods, services and factors of production (labor, land, and capital) is not only a necessary condition for capitalism but, as noted in the previous chapter, part of its very definition.

Although commerce per se may be necessary for capitalism, it is certainly not a sufficient condition for it. In tribal and poor agricultural societies, both internal and external trade has existed, although at low levels.[14] Some assert that such early trade differed significantly from modern trade because it was embedded in society,

---

[14] See Frederic L. Pryor, *The Origins of the Economy: A Comparative Study of Distribution in Primitive and Peasant Economies* (New York: Academic Press, 1977); and *Economic Systems of Foraging, Agricultural, and Industrial Societies* (New York: Cambridge University Press, 2005).

so that such factors as kinship, religious relations, political ties, etc. were its primary determinants.[15] This argument seems overdrawn because serious questions can be raised about the relative importance of such noneconomic factors in early trade, especially for goods from faraway places. Moreover, even today, these social factors play a certain role in constraining and structuring the activities of merchants (although many might claim they are only acting "in enlightened self interest").

The Asian and European countries under consideration had profit-oriented trade (misleadingly designated by some as "commercial capitalism") for many centuries, even though by 1700 such market trade did not account for a sufficient share of the total production to qualify their economies as capitalist. Nevertheless, by the beginning of the eighteenth century, northwestern Europe, China, India, and Japan all had highly active markets for goods, and, thus, had institutions that could facilitate capitalism.

---

[15] This thesis has been advanced with especial vigor by Karl Polanyi and his followers. It is irrelevant to my argument that reciprocity, gift-giving, and other types of nonmarket exchange, on which Polanyi focuses so much attention, may have been more important in these tribal and low-level agricultural societies than in modern societies.

Origins of Capitalism

With the exception of one country, the large Asian nations and northwestern Europe also had active labor markets, with large pools of unbound workers who could be employed for productive purposes. The exception was India, whose caste system limited occupational and geographical mobility.

Land markets were less active than the markets for goods and labor; nevertheless, markets for land existed in all the countries under examination. Reliable evidence also suggests that such markets in land were freer and more active in China than in Europe at the beginning of the eighteenth century.[16]

Finally, qualitative differences in capital markets between East and West were apparently slight.[17] All of the countries under consideration had money, banks, and certain sophisticated financial instruments such as bills of exchange. In the eighteenth century the banking

---

[16] Pomeranz, *op. cit.*, Chapter 2.

[17] Evidence on banking systems comes from: Frank Perlin, "Financial Institutions and Business Practices across the Euro-Asian Interface: Comparative and Structural Considerations, 1500–1900." In Hans Pohl, ed., *The European Discovery of the World and Its Economic Effects on Pre-Industrial Society, 1500–1900* (Stuttgart: Steiner Verlag, 1990), 257–304; and Hugh Patrick, "Japan: 1868–1914." In Rondo Cameron, et al., eds., *Banking in the Early Stages of Industrialization* (New York: Oxford University Press, 1967) 239–930.

systems of India and China appeared in many respects the equal of Europe's, and some argue that Japan's banking system was not far behind. I provide evidence below, however, that such capital markets may have been considerably more active in Europe than in Asia.

In brief, the presence of markets did not particularly favor one county over another as the birthplace of capitalism.

2. Urbanization

a. Direct Impacts of Urbanization. For extensive trade in goods to occur, a central market place is necessary (at least it was before the invention of e-commerce), and this requires a certain degree of urbanization. Trade fairs can, of course, take place outside heavily urban areas. In the twelfth and thirteenth centuries, for example, such fairs were held in several villages in the fiefdoms of Champagne and Brie in central France, an area strategically located on routes connecting Normandy, England, the Baltic area, and the Low Countries with cities in Italy. Nevertheless, towns or cities – defined by the presence of full-time craftsmen and a division of labor – are generally required for trade to become important in the daily lives of ordinary people.

But urbanization alone does not guarantee the emergence of capitalism. Although town life does not have as long a pedigree as trade, cities have existed for at least four millennia. Many ancient cities represented islands of capitalism: trade in goods, services, and factors of production was extensive within their walls, and the other conditions of capitalism discussed in the previous chapter, including security of property, were met. Nevertheless, except for a slight commercialization of the rural areas, these activities had little additional influence on the economy of the hinterland, where the overwhelming bulk of the population lived. Although the countryside traded food for urban goods, trade in other goods was small in proportion to the total production, and slavery or serfdom, rather than labor markets, often served to allocate labor. In brief, the nation as a whole did not have a capitalist economic system.

One way to assess the influence of city life on the development of capitalism is to compare the degree of urbanization at particular points in time with the date at which a country passed the threshold of capitalism. The available data for Europe, set out in Table 3–1 above, show no significant relationship between urbanization in various years in the eighteenth century and the capitalist threshold year.[18]

[18] More specifically, I employed both a Kendall rank order approach and an ordinary least squares regression to find any relationship, but without success. Bairoch, *op. cit.* (1988), p. 261, has a table of 18 countries showing the "start of modern

This result can be interpreted to mean that urbanization by itself is not a sufficient condition for capitalism.

The available data also suggests that at the beginning of the nineteenth century, urbanization was somewhat lower in Asian countries than in northwestern Europe (although Asia was not lower than other European nations). For instance, Paul Bairoch estimates that the urbanization ratio of China fell from roughly 11 to 14 percent at the beginning of the sixteenth century to 6.0 to 7.5 percent by the 1840s and asserts that the difference in urbanization between China and India was not great, and that India showed a similar decline in urbanization between 1700 and 1800.[19] Declining urbanization indicates falling agricultural productivity. That is to say, cities were shrinking because fewer urban dwellers could be supported by the food produced by a farmer in the rural sector. This is a sign of diminishing returns to the land (discussed below), which acted as a brake to the development of capitalism.

b. Indirect Impacts of Urbanization. In recent decades a number of historians have argued that

[economic] development" and the level of urbanization at that time. Again, neither Kendall rank order nor ordinary least squares approaches showed a significant relationship between these two variables.

[19] Bairoch, *op. cit.*, pp. 356–58, 430.

capitalism really originated in England in the rural, rather than in the urban, sector. Two aspects of this argument deserve mention.[20]

Some emphasize that in the seventeenth and eighteenth centuries industrial production in England began to be relocated in rural areas either to escape guild regulations or to have access to the power generated by a water wheel. But the workers in such manufacturing plants appear to have accounted for only a very small share of total nonagricultural production of goods; moreover, the entrepreneurial drive establishing such enterprises came mainly from the urban sector.

Robert Brenner has made a different and more forceful argument, focusing on the impact in England of the trade in foodstuffs between the cities and the rural areas. Such trade was accompanied in England by the consolidation of farms in the sixteenth and seventeenth centuries, when traditional land tenure arrangements were transformed. Landlords merged fields and then rented out most of their land at a fixed amount to commercially-oriented

---

[20] See Trevor Henry Aston and C.H.E. Philpin, *The Brenner Debate: Agrarian Class Structure and Economic Development in Pre-Industrial Europe* (New York: Cambridge University Press, 1985). In the next paragraph I refer to Robert Brenner, "Agrarian Class Structure and Economic Development in Pre-Industrial Europe," pp. 10–63 in Aston and Philpin, *op. cit.*

("capitalist") farmers, who either worked the land them-selves or used hired laborers. After removing the subsis-tence of the capitalist farmers and their wage payment of their workers, the remainder was then sold to the urban areas. These farmers thus had a strong incentive to raise labor productivity in order to increase their income from sales to the city, and this, in turn, required capital accumulation.

Appendix 3–2 provides further discussion of the Brenner thesis, and reveals several arguments that raise problems. Higher labor productivity in agriculture, result-ing from improved methods of production, is certainly necessary for capitalism since it permits greater produc-tion of other goods by releasing labor from the rural sector. Nevertheless, production of manufactured goods and availability of foreign goods must also increase at the same time, or else relative prices would turn against agriculture, and the enhanced agricultural productivity might not pay off. Furthermore, commercialization of the countryside and expansion of trade by themselves do not necessarily bring increased productivity or capital-ism. The producers must be able to finance their innova-tions and capital equipment and reap the rewards – that is, not have them expropriated by landowners (through rent hikes), tax authorities, or church officials. Given such prerequisites, it should be clear that improvements in agricultural productivity alone were not in themselves a sufficient stimulus to bring forth capitalism.

3. Security of Private Property and Enforcement of Contract

If property is not secure from the depredations of invading forces, governments (central or local), or neighbors, investment to increase productivity will obviously be discouraged. Involved in the security of property are a variety of institutions, both public and private, that constrain the coercive ability of those other than the formal owners of the physical or intellectual capital involved. Some economic historians interpret the entire "rise of the West" in terms of the various ways in which governments and other organizations made private property and contracts more secure, giving people wishing to become wealthy an incentive to innovate, invest, and participate in the market economy.[21]

How can we test this idea? Objective indicators, such as the laws limiting the actions of government or the establishment of police to prevent theft, are imperfect: governments may disregard the laws, and police

[21] Douglas C. North and Robert Paul Thomas, *The Rise of the Western World: A New Economic History* (Cambridge: Cambridge University Press, 1973).

may be ineffective because of such perennial factors in human society as corruption or incompetence. We sometimes read of the sanctity of property and contract in eighteenth-century England, but detailed local histories covering legal matters at that time suggest that actual practices were far from ideal.[22] We also hear that in Japan and China, property was considered sacred or that, conversely, in India merchants were at the mercy of the state.[23] Unfortunately, it is unclear how secure, or insecure, property actually was in any of these nations. What we need is a measure that reflects how people on the ground viewed the security of their property.

We cannot, of course, interview eighteenth century entrepreneurs, nor do we have systematic accounts of their daily activities. As a way of gauging how confident people felt about investing their money in the long run, we can look at some proxy indicator, such as interest rates. More specifically, insecure property relations

---

[22] A useful summary is provided by Patrick O'Brien, "Central Government and the Economy, 1688–1815." In Roderick Floud and Donald McCloskey, eds., *The Economic History of Britain since 1700*, 2nd edition (New York: Cambridge University Press, 1994), 205–42.

[23] Fernand Braudel, *Civilization and Capitalism, 15th–18th Century*, vol. 3, *The Perspective of the World*, trans., Siân Reynolds (New York: Harper & Row, 1984 [1979]), 520. He adds, however, that Indian capitalists were not impotent against the state.

léad to higher interest rates to compensate lenders for the additional risk they are assuming.

The interest rate is also affected in the long term by the manner in which contracts are enforced, and in this case a variety of institutions, both public and private, play a role. For instance, in collectivistic societies, private institutions, such as clan sanctions, may be involved, while in individualistic societies, contract enforcement may be more of a governmental function.[24] Moreover, short-term interest rates are also affected by a variety of immediate supply and demand factors, such as business cycle conditions, civil unrest, harvest failures that create the sudden need for cash, or sudden restrictions on their activities (for instance, legal limits on interest rates). But by averaging interest rates over long periods, the impact of short-run considerations is very much reduced, and we gain a picture of the long-run security of property and the enforcement of contract.[25]

Unfortunately, measuring interest rates is not simple because in any particular time period, they vary according

---

[24] Avner Greif in "Coercion and Exchange: How Did Markets Evolve?" (2008) http://ssrn.com/abstract-1304204 offers a useful discussion of both security of property and enforcement of contract and their interrelationships.

[25] Although long-term usury restrictions might affect average interest rates over a long period, they could be circumvented in many different ways, so their impact is difficult to judge.

Table 3-2. *Average Long-Term Nominal Commercial Interest Rates for Selected Countries in the Seventeenth and Eighteenth Centuries*

Country	Seventeenth Century		Eighteenth Century		Data Quality
	First Half	Second Half	First Half	Second Half	
Europe and North America					
England	6.0–10.0%	4.0–6.0%	4.7%	3.2%	Good
France	8.2	5.0–8.2	5.6	5.5	Fair
Germany	< – – – –	4.0–5.0	– – – >	—	Poor
Italy	< – – – –	4.0–5.0	– – – >	—	Poor
Netherlands	6.7	5.3	3.5	6.3	Fair
Russia	4.5–10.0	5.0–10.0	—	—	Poor
Sweden	—	7.5	4.6	4.1	Fair
United States	—	—	5.0–8.0	5.4–10.0	Poor
Asia					
China	36–60	< – – – –	10–36	– – – >	Poor
India	17.8	13.5	9.4	– – – >	Good
Japan	—	10.0–50.0	4.6–12.5	2.9–9.7	Poor/fair

Notes: Sources of nominal interest rate data and other notes are given in Appendix 3–1. A dash indicates that no data are available. Price series for these various countries are not very comparable, but as far as I could tell, annual average price increases were sufficiently low to make these nominal interest rates roughly approximate to price-adjusted (real) interest rates.

to the status of the borrower, the length of the loan, the position of the lender, or the part of the country in which the transaction takes place. Moreover, interest rate data are also not readily available for all years. Nevertheless, we can, for our purposes, make certain rough approximations.

Table 3–2 presents data on the average interest rates on long-term loans in selected countries for half-century periods from 1600 to 1800. Since the price levels during these half-century periods were roughly constant in most countries, such data also roughly reflect price-adjusted interest rates.

The data strongly suggest that interest rates during the seventeenth and eighteenth centuries were lower in northwestern Europe than in China, India, or Japan. As a result, we may tentatively conclude that property was more secure and contracts were more enforced in northwestern Europe than in the three Asian nations and, as a result, that investment conditions were more favorable there for capitalism to develop.

4. Education[26]

Both economic development in general and capitalism in particular require that a significant share of the

---

[26] The sources used in this discussion are Margaret C. Jacob, *Scientific Culture and the Making of the Industrial West* (New York: Oxford

population be literate. Literacy is crucial for inventors to profit from the discoveries of others; for managers to keep up with new products and processes, not to mention with the world of commerce; for merchants to operate their businesses; and for workers to learn how to operate and repair their machines. And it is not just reading per se but also the written communication between these varied groups that is important.

Although extensive trade or production of goods on any scale larger than a handicraft workshop requires both literacy and numeracy, the minimum amount of literacy needed is a controversial issue. Some have argued that most of the early factory jobs required

University Press, 1997); Joel Mokyr, *The Gifts of Athena: Historical Origins of the Knowledge Economy* (Princeton NJ: Princeton University Press, 2002); Jack Goody, *Capitalism and Modernity: The Great Debate* (Malden, MA: Polity Press, 2004); John A. Hall, "States and Societies: The Miracle in Comparative Perspective." In Baechler, Hall, and Mann, eds., *op. cit.*, pp. 20–39; and Michael Sanderson, "Literacy and Social Mobility in the Industrial Revolution in England," *Past and Present* 56 (August 1972): 75–104. Other sources include Frederic L. Pryor, *Economic Systems of Foraging, Agricultural, and Industrial Societies, op. cit.*, Chapter 5; Evelyn Sakakida Rawski, *Education and Popular Literacy in Ch'ing China* (Ann Arbor: University of Michigan Press, 1979); and Carlo M. Cipolla, *Literacy and Development in the West* (Hammondsworth, U.K.: Penguin, 1969).

little education.[27] Several European countries that had passed the capitalist threshold in the nineteenth century (such as Italy and Spain) had literacy rates well below 50 percent. Still, the average level of literacy in a nation in the nineteenth century was significantly related to the year in which it reached a noticeable level of industrialization. Perhaps a minimum level of literacy is necessary for capitalism to begin, and once capitalism is underway, the literacy rate increases rapidly thereafter.

Measuring literacy is also tricky. One common indicator is the ability of people to write their names on a document, such as a wedding certificate. But a signature does not really tell us if the signer can read. Alternatively, we might judge literacy levels from the share of people who have had at least a specified number of years of schooling, but comparable data on schooling are difficult to obtain, especially since much schooling was informal and private. For nonphonetic languages such as Chinese, a person might know the hundreds of characters necessary to

---

[27] For instance, Michael Sanderson, "Literacy and Social Mobility in the Industrial Revolution in England," *Past and Present* 1972, vol. 56 (August): 75–104. The relation of literacy and industrialization is presented in Frederic L. Pryor. *Economic Systems of Foraging, Agricultural, and Industrial Societies, op. cit.*, Chapter 5.

Table 3–3. *Adult Literacy Rates in the Nineteenth Century*

Country	Date	Share of Adult Population Who Could Read
Europe and North America		
Austro-Hungary	1851	55–60%
Belgium	1856	50–55
England/Wales	1851	67–70
Denmark	c1850	>70
France	1851	55–60
Prussia	1849	80
Italy	c1850	20–25
Netherlands	c1850	>70
Russia	c1850	<50
Scotland	1851	80
Spain	1857	25
Sweden	1850	90
Switzerland	c1850	>70
United States	1850	76–84
Asia		
China	1880	c. 25%
India	1921	c. 5%
Japan	1868	c. 25–30%

Notes: Literacy is defined solely in terms of reading ability. The data are also not completely comparable. The data for Europe come primarily from Carlo M. Cipolla, *Literacy and Development in the West, op. cit.* (1969), Tables 21 and 23. The estimate for the United States is rough and includes slaves. In China, roughly 30 to 45 percent of all males attended school and presumably possessed functional literacy skills, whereas probably less than 10 percent of girls were literate, according to Evelyn Sakakida Rawsky, "Functional Literacy in the Nineteenth Century." In Daniel P. Resnick ed., *Literacy in Historical Perspective*. Washington: Library of Congress, 1983, 85–105. In Japan at the time of the Meiji Restoration, somewhat more than 40 percent of Japanese boys and about 10 percent of girls were getting some kind formal education outside of their homes, according to the estimates of Ronald Dore, *Education in Tokugawa Japan* (Berkeley, CA: University of California Press, 1965), 254. The data for India come from Syed Nurullah and J. P. Naik, A *Student's History of Education in India, 1800–1965*, 5th rev. ed., (Bombay: Macmillan, 1964), 272.

operate a business and write simple business letters, and yet not be able to read a book.[28]

Table 3–3 presents a rough picture of literacy in the middle of the nineteenth century, where literacy is defined as the ability to read and understand a text. Since it is hard to define "read and understand," these data must be viewed only as approximations.

Despite the crudeness of the data, however, it appears that literacy was considerably higher in northwestern Europe (and throughout the continent) than in China, India, and Japan. On the other hand, literacy levels in China and Japan were roughly similar to those in Italy and Spain, which had passed the capitalist threshold year by around 1880 (Table 3–1). This suggests that China and Japan had sufficient literacy to permit the development of capitalism, while in India the potential for capitalism was lower because the literacy rate was so small.

Literacy per se may not, however, be the crucial variable. Scholarly societies and their publications have played a key role in the spread of information about advances in technology and science. Britain's Royal Society was founded in 1662, and a variety of similar organizations sprang up all over Europe in the succeeding century. In China, India, and Japan, however, such groups were not

[28] Rawsky, *op. cit.*

organized until several hundred years later, a state of affairs that retarded the flow of new science and technology. In India, the Brahmins treated advances in math and astronomy as caste secrets, scientific knowledge diffused more slowly, and, as a result, the society could not quickly take advantage of these new discoveries.[29] And in China, scholars were remote from the technical artisans and considered "theory" suitable for gentlemen, "practice" for the common folk.

In brief, once a nation has attained a certain level of literacy, the institutions helping to spread scientific and technical knowledge are a crucial factor in the transformation of an economy to capitalism. This was an important factor in the rise of capitalism in northwestern Europe.

C. The Role of Government

Three key questions to ask about the influence of government on the origins of capitalism need to be asked: What was the role of political freedom? What was the role of

---

[29] This statement is based on the analysis of Hall, *op. cit.* The generalization about China is based on Joseph Needham, *The Great Titration: Science and Society in East and West* (London: Allen & Unwin, 1969), 142.

political centralization? What was the role of active governmental incentives?

1. Was Capitalism Born in Free Societies?

In the popular press we sometimes come across the claim that political freedom gave birth to capitalism. (The reverse causation, proposed by some prominent economists, is discussed in Chapter 6.) Let's look at the evidence.

Appendix 3–4 tabulates the twenty-four independent nations that can be considered as capitalist in the nineteenth century, listed according to the date of their estimated capitalism threshold year (see Table 3–1). To measure their degree of political freedom, I use the Polity 2 variable of Marshall and Jaggers, a measure for politically independent nations that extends back to 1800.[30] Although this statistic actually measures democracy, it is highly correlated with political freedom in cross-section regressions and can serve as a useful proxy. It ranges from −10 (autocratic) to +10 (democratic).

In the nineteenth century, there is a twenty-year period before various nations can be considered capitalist in

---

[30] Monty Marshall and Keith Jaggers, *Polity IV Project: Political Regime Characteristics and Transitions, 1800–2004*, www.cidem.umd.edu/polity (2005).

which the average degree of political freedom was −4.71, which is quite low. For the nations that did become capitalist before the end of the nineteenth century, the average degree of political freedom was −4.01. In brief, capitalism seemed to begin in countries with only slightly less autocracy (more freedom) than was typical at the time.

2. Capitalism and Political Centralization?

Some political scientists claim that political decentralization (or fragmentation) was a necessary but not sufficient condition for the transition to capitalism, and at least one historian has added that the merchants must also play an important role in political affairs for the development of capitalism.[31] Since it is generally believed that the governments of China, India, and Japan were more centralized and that their merchants played a far less important political role than in northwestern Europe, capitalism was less likely to originate in the former than in the latter group of nations. We must, however, examine some relevant evidence before accepting this argument.

As discussed below, capitalism cannot take hold unless the government is sufficiently centralized to provide law

---

[31] John A. Hall. "States and Societies: The Miracle in Comparative Perspective." In Jean Baechler, John A. Hall, and Michael Mann, *op. cit.* pp. 20–39.

and order, protect private property, and reduce internal trade barriers. But when political centralization reaches the point where the ruling elite can easily expropriate private property of rich merchants and manufacturers or take other actions with similar adverse impacts on economic activities, the development of capitalism is discouraged. The degree to which such governmental activities were possible in the various countries under discussion, however, is unclear. Modern scholarship has only recently begun to study in earnest the civil law in China and in some of the other Asian nations to determine the extent of various legal constraints on what the governmental could do in the economy.[32]

Political centralization can also limit the mobility of labor, either directly by returning escaped workers who are legally bound to an employer, or indirectly, by allowing employers to force these escaped workers to return. In some northwest European nations, an escaped worker who fled to a town and remained there for a year and a day became a free man (*Stadtluft macht frei* – city air brings freedom), a legal loophole not found in Asian nations.

---

[32] See Kathryn Bernhardt and Philip C.C. Huang, eds., *Civil Law in Qing and Republican China* (Stanford, CA: Stanford University Press, 1994).

Paralleling the relative political decentralization in northwestern European nations was the rise from the late twelfth century onward of the semi-autonomous city, where the commercial elite exercised considerable political power. This occurred in large part because of the strongly organized merchant guilds. Although Asia too had such guilds, they were much weaker than their European counterparts.[33] Even after the consolidation of the state in northwestern Europe, the merchant elite continued to maintain its power, particularly since most kings were dependent on loans from private financiers. For instance, at the end of the twelfth century, England's King Richard I could not raise the funds for a standing army of even three hundred knights, and in the early fourteenth century, King Edward III would not have been able to finance his war against France without the aid of Italian bankers. In contrast, the Chinese emperors had no need to borrow and could mobilize almost one million soldiers without borrowing through taxes and forced contributions.

The power of the European merchants over military operations and the establishment of colonies served to

---

[33] Discussion in this and the following paragraph is drawn from Eric H. Mielants, *The Origins of Capitalism and the Rise of the West* (2007), *op. cit.*, p. 47, pp. 70–78.

increase international trade. This stands in stark contrast to the actions of the Ming emperors, who, between 1371 and 1567, severely curtailed foreign trade, closed the governmental navy yards, allowed the ships and the shipbuilding industry to deteriorate, and forbade Chinese merchants from traveling abroad for commercial purposes. No European king could have implemented such policies, and the relative feebleness of European monarchies created an opening in which capitalism could emerge. As one economic historian has argued, "The political power of the wealthy merchant class, an urban-based bourgeoisie, was a *sine qua non* for the creation of a capitalist system."[34]

3. Governmental Actions Favoring Commerce

One extreme of governmental attitudes toward commerce is represented by the late Ming dynasty (1368–1644). According to one economic historian, "There is no evidence that the Ming government spent funds on road maintenance and construction, apart from erecting the stone bridges outside Peking ... [It made] no effort ... to increase efficiency of the imperial postal

---

[34] Eric H. Mielants, *op. cit.*, p. 78.

system."[35] This scholar further notes that merchandise transport was hindered by the frequent roadblocks set up along trade routes and by tolls for the use of the Grand Canal. Regarding other aspects of expenditure policies, he remarks that "as the Ming administrators saw it, to promote those advanced sectors of the economy would only widen the economic imbalance [between sectors], which in turn would threaten the empire's political unity." This attitude was reinforced by the attempt of the Ming emperors "to prevent the regions from over-developing any financial potential of their own, and thus from challenging the central government." Such anti-developmental attitudes carried over to the Qing dynasty (1644–1912) as well.

Governmental influence on capital accumulation, either positive or negative, was also manifested in other ways. For instance, Joseph Needham, a prominent historian, argues that "the despising of the merchant was a very old characteristic in Chinese thought ... capital accumulation in Chinese society there could indeed be, but the application of it in permanently productive industrial enterprises was constantly inhibited by the scholar-

[35] The citations in this paragraph are from Ray Huang, *Taxation and Governmental Finance in Sixteenth-Century Ming China* (New York: Cambridge University Press, 1974), 2, 317–21.

bureaucrats, as indeed any other social action which might threaten their supremacy. Thus, the merchant guilds in China never approached the status and power of the merchant guilds in the city-states of European civilization."[36] For capitalism to arise, government needs to provide "traditional" public goods. These include the creation and maintenance of transportation infrastructure that permit the buyers and sellers of goods and services physically to reach the marketplace, such as roads, canals, and harbors. In the sixteenth century, England was already sufficiently centralized to have an impressive network of roads and water transport.[37] Equally important for the emergence of capitalism, internal trade barriers, such as private tolls, should be minimal; this was a condition that existed in England but not in most other Western European nations (not in France, for example). Another important public good is a police force to maintain domestic order and safety. Since many current developing economies have these government-provided services and yet do not have capitalist economic systems, it is obvious that these services do not guarantee the

---

[36] Joseph Needham, *op. cit.*, p. 184, 197.
[37] Evelyn Wood, *The Origins of Capitalism: A Longer View* (New York: Verso, 2002), 99 ff.

emergence of capitalism. But without them, capitalism cannot appear.

Governmental policies aimed at reducing the costs of foreign trade, such as offering subsidies to the shipbuilding industry or sponsoring military adventures to establish colonies, are also important to the origins of capitalism. Some scholars argue that foreign trade based on exploitation of colonial riches can by itself ignite capitalism; they point out that China, Japan, and India did not have colonies on any extensive scale, whereas Europe did. But economically exploited colonies have existed for many centuries without capitalism developing in the mother country. And although colonial trade may have provided crucial investment funds for the development of capitalism in England (a dubious and hotly debated proposition), this did not appear the case in some countries, such as Spain and Portugal, which had much more colonial trade than England. In brief, colonial trade per se does not account for the origin of capitalism. A particular kind of colonial trade did play an important role, however, and receives comment below.

Japan appeared to have had fewer restrictions on foreign trade and commercial activities than China.[38] After

---

[38] Although Tokugawa Japan was alleged to have a "policy of national exclusion" (*sakoku*) that discouraged foreign trade, some

the Meiji Restoration (1862), the government also took many positive steps to encourage development and modernize the economy. It is not by accident that Japan was the first of the three Asian countries under consideration to develop capitalism.

In sum, just as in today's world, particular governmental actions can encourage or discourage the development of capitalism. The motivations behind these actions require an analysis of the political environment of these nations, which lies outside the scope of this book.

D. Social and Personal Factors

Early in the twentieth century, the famous sociologist Max Weber made a strong argument linking capitalism with the development of Protestantism.[39] Many aspects

have recently argued that this is an exaggeration of Tokugawan policies and that Japan conducted a certain amount of trade with neighboring countries, as well as with the Dutch East India Company. For other countries there were, however, certain restrictions. Sources on this topic include Kazui Tashiro, "Foreign Trade in the Tokugawa Period – Particularly with Korea." In Akira Hayami, Osamu Saitô, and Ronald P. Toby, eds., *Emergence of Economic Society in Japan 1600–1859*, vol. 1 (New York: Oxford University Press, 2003), 105–18.

[39] Max Weber, *The Protestant Ethic and the Spirit of Capitalism*, translated by Talcott Parsons (New York: Routledge 1930 [1905]). Kurt

Capitalism Reassessed

of his argument have subsequently been discredited. As
one commentator notes, the "Protestant ethic" of hard
work, austerity, thrift, and accumulation has been found
among the Jains in India, Confucians in China, Wahabis
in the near East, and merchant groups in Japan and other
countries. Others have pointed out that the ambition of
some groups to accumulate capital and become rich can
be found all over the world. Some historians also claim
that the capitalist mentality was found on large agricultural estates in Europe after the ninth century and that
many merchant groups and estate owners in Europe had
"capitalist values" as early as the fourteenth century.

Nevertheless, the core idea of Weber's argument still
commands attention, namely, that a change in the mentality of a significant share of the population is required
for capitalism to develop. Certainly the climate for capitalism seems unfavorable in peasant societies, where collective solidarity is more valued than individualism (so

Samuelsson, *Religion and Economic Action; A Critique of Max Weber,*
translated by E. Geoffrey French (New York, Harper & Row, 1964)
presents a comprehensive critique of Weber. In this paragraph
I have also drawn upon arguments by Jack Goody, *Capitalism
and Modernity: The Great Debate* (Malden, MA: Polity Press,
2004); H. E. Hallam, "The Medieval Social Picture." In Eugene
Kamenka and R. S. Neale, eds., *Feudalism, Capitalism and Beyond*
(Canberra: Australian National University Press, 1973), 29–64;
and Eric Mielants, *op. cit.*, pp. 21–22.

that land is held by a group, not by individuals); where magic and myths, rather than rational thought, dominate the thinking about the world; where profit seeking is considered grubby and trade and manufacturing are held to be unworthy occupations for gentlemen; and where leisure is more highly prized than ownership of fancy goods. In addition, certain social practices have negative impacts on economic activity, for instance, caste distinctions in India or the binding of women's feet in China, both of which reduces the labor force available for particular work outside the home.

Arguments about the "spirit of capitalism" raise a key issue: it may not necessarily be the character traits or values of an entire population that are important to the origins of capitalism but rather, those among an elite and active minority. If this latter group chooses to seek glory, rather than riches, it is doubtful that capitalism will arise and thrive. The idea of the "sweetness of trade" (*douceur de commerce*), that is, the idea that riches gained through trade and production are more desirable than glory and loot gained from warfare, took centuries to gain general acceptance even in Europe.[40] And not until it did was capitalism fully established.

---

[40] Albert O. Hirschman, *The Passions and the Interests: Political Arguments for Capitalism before Its Triumph* (Princeton, NJ: Princeton University Press, 1997).

How do we trace the effect of values and attitudes on the development of capitalism? And how do we measure values and attitudes in the first place, especially when we are dealing with the past? My own attempt to explore the relationship between values and capitalism in recent years starts with the 1999–2002 World Value Survey.[41] From this source I selected sixty-six questions that seemed most directly related to the economy and calculated the correlation between each of them and the degree of capitalism in the various OECD nations (discussed in Chapter 2 and Appendix 2–2). For slightly more than half of the individual values I discovered a statistically significant relationship with the degree of capitalism. However, when this calculation was repeated and per capita GDP was held constant, I found a significant relationship for only 6 percent of the values with capitalism, and none of these values appeared central to the economic system. For the thirty-seven values for which survey data on almost all countries in the sample are available, I extracted the five most common underlying "components" and correlated

[41] Ronald Inglehart, Miguel Basáñez, Jaime Díez-Medrano, Loek Halman, and Ruud Luijkx, *Human Beliefs and Values: A Cross-Cultural Sourcebook Based on the 1999–2002 Value Surveys* (Mexico City: Siglo XXI Editores, 2004).

these with the degree of capitalism in each country. No statistically significant relationships, however, emerged.[42] In brief, the relationship between the degree of capitalism in a given nation and the values of its population do not seem very important.

We might interpret this failure to link values and the overall degree of capitalism in several ways. As mentioned above, the values of a small group of people seeking renown either though military exploits or entrepreneurial activities might be much more important to the development of capitalism than are the values of the population as a whole. Or, it may be that, when capitalism was developing in the eighteenth and nineteenth centuries, the nations differed more in their values than now. Had the World Value Study been conducted two centuries ago, we would perhaps have seen more striking contrasts between the values of nations that developed capitalism early and those that did not. Or the questions

---

[42] More technically, I carried out a principal component analysis of the 37 values for the countries in the sample. This statistical procedure extracts different sets of the common elements (components) for the values under consideration. From the five most important components, I then calculated the individual scores of each country. Finally, I calculated the correlation of these component scores with the capitalism scores for the countries, but found no statistically significant relationships.

in this public opinion poll might not have reflected the values that were important for the development of capitalism. For instance, in earlier centuries merchants and others engaged in making money did not have a very high social standing in certain societies, such as China and India, and such attitudes undoubtedly discouraged ambitious young people from entering these fields; unfortunately, the World Value Study had no questions about attitudes toward trade, manufacturing, and wealth. Or, finally, causation may run in the opposite direction. That is, capitalism, even of a relatively low degree, may lead to changes in values, and not the other way around. The question remains open.

If values cannot clearly account for the emergence of capitalist per se or how rapidly it advances in a nation, they do seem to influence the style of capitalism that develops. In Chapter 5, I am able to link economic values in various industrialized nations with their particular type of capitalism, rather than with their degree of capitalism. Moreover, other scholars have also found relationships between some values and long-run economic development. For instance, Stefan Voigt and San-Min Park use data from a study of the values of managers in various countries to show that the productivity of capital and labor combined (total factor productivity) is positively related to the degree to which the respondents value individual responsibility and negatively related to their desire to avoid uncertainty.[43] These positive results are suggestive, but given the enormous statistical problems that are involved in exploring these issues, we will not know for a long time exactly how values are related to the degree of capitalism.

E. Environmental Conditions

In the eighteenth century, Europe, China, and Japan all faced roughly similar environmental problems of diminishing returns to land and shortages of fuel (wood), fibers, and building materials.[44] In a provocative book, Kenneth Pomeranz argues that in the nineteenth

---

[43] Stefan Voigt and San-Min Park, "Values and Norms Matter: On the Basic Determinants of Long-Run Economic Development," http://ssrn.com/abstract=1165343 (2008).

[44] Pomeranz, *op. cit.*, Chapter 5. Although the conventional wisdom is that diminishing returns to the land were strictly an Asian problem, many recent works point to seriously diminishing returns to agricultural land in Europe from the fourteenth century onward. See, for example, Emannuel Le Roy Ladurie, *The Peasants of Languedoc*, trans. John Day (Urbana: University of Illinois Press, 1974); or Douglass C. North and Robert Paul Thomas (*The Rise of the Western World: A New Economic History*. (New York: Cambridge: University Press, 1973).

century further environmental difficulties, sidestepped in Europe, became worse in Asia, so that further economic development of the latter countries was severely constrained.[45] Let's explore this hypothesis.

As shown in Table 3–1, urbanization remained the same or rose in most European nations in the eighteenth century, while in China and India, urbanization was on the wane. These two countries seemed to have a decline in agricultural productivity, which meant that a given number of farmers could support fewer city dwellers. In contrast, agricultural productivity in northwestern Europe was increasing, due in part to the introduction of new crop rotation systems, new types of plants, and new irrigation methods.

In the eighteenth and nineteenth centuries, Europe also began a large-scale substitution of readily available coal for wood as a fuel to heat its homes and provide power for its factories. But coal in China was located in remote regions in the north and northwest and, because of transport and other difficulties, could not as easily serve as a substitute for wood. For other reasons, use of coal in Japan and India was also delayed. This meant that forest lands were disappearing more quickly in these three Asian countries, a development

[45] Pomeranz, *op. cit.*

that resulted in more soil erosion and other obstacles to agriculture.[46]

Similarly Europe – especially England – was able to obtain fibers for textile production from the New World, whereas the Asian countries had to transfer valuable lands that had once been used for cultivating food to the growing of fibrous plants or pastures for sheep. Europe was also able to obtain a rising share of its food calories from its trade with the New World, first in the form of sugar and later, in the nineteenth century, in the form of grains and dried meat. Northwestern Europe's trade with the New World, especially after 1830, led to imports of land-intensive products that allowed it to circumvent diminishing returns in agriculture. Moreover, northwestern Europe more quickly adopted crops from the New World, such as potatoes, which allowed it to economize further on land use. Thus, it was not trade per se that aided the rise of capitalism in northwestern Europe, but trade in products that overcame environmental constraints.

---

[46] The critical role of coal in industrialization and the development of capitalism in northwestern Europe is emphasized by other historians, such as E.A. Wrigley, "The Divergence of England: The Growth of the English Economy in the Seventeenth and Eighteenth Centuries," *Transactions of the Royal Historical Society*, 10, 6th series (2000): 117–41.

Rather than focusing on new technologies or on importing certain land-intensive crops, China, India, and Japan tried to raise the productivity of land by employing more labor-intensive means of production. Although this strategy did lead to greater production, productivity per agricultural worker fell because of diminishing returns. It was coal and colonies that underlay the economic divergence between northwestern Europe and Asia in the nineteenth century.[47]

F. Pulling Things Together

The quest for the origins of capitalism is hindered by the lack of adequate historical data that would permit a rigorous testing of hypotheses. Even for England, with its well-documented history base, fierce debates still rage over the importance of the various causal factors. Nevertheless, we can draw some tentative conclusions.

Northwestern Europe had an edge over China, India, and Japan in the early development of capitalism in the eighteenth and nineteen centuries because it had a higher level of economic development. This advantage eased the development of capitalism, especially when supported by complementary institutions. Northwestern Europe

---

[47] Pomeranz, *op.cit.*

also appeared to have an advantage over the three Asian nations in these institutions, especially those protecting private property and aiding the spread of scientific and technological knowledge. Other institutional conditions favorable to the development of capitalism present a mixed picture. For instance, in the eighteenth century, Europe did not have a significant edge in markets for goods, labor, land, and capital. Although my discussion above focuses those institutions that I believe to be most important, many other institutions in the private sector may, also have played a role in the origins of capitalism, such as joint stock companies, which facilitate the amassing of capital from many different sources and its maintenance over many years. These institutions do not, however, appear to be crucial in explaining why capitalism arose in northwestern Europe and not in China, India, and Japan.[48]

[48] Timur Kuran, *The Long Divergence: How Islamic Law Held Back the Middle East op. cit.*, discusses this point in a fascinating study of Middle East economies, where only temporary partnerships were recognized in the middle ages, so that when a partner died or wished to pull out, the assets of the partnership would have to be liquidated for the investor to be recompensed. Capital accumulation was further discouraged because Islamic inheritance law required the spreading of the deceased's wealth among many heirs (particularly in polygamous marriages). This meant that one heir could not reform the partnership with share of capital he

The role of government also seems to be an important factor in the origins of capitalism. In northwestern Europe governments were more encouraging to trade and production and the commercial elite played a greater role in setting governmental policy than in China, India, and Japan. Governments in the former area were also less centralized, and they exercised fewer arbitrary powers in the economy than those in the three Asian countries.

It is difficult to draw definite conclusions about the relative impact of social and cultural factors in the development of capitalism in East and West. On the other hand, the evidence regarding environmental conditions seems clear: in the nineteenth century these were more favorable to the growth of capitalism in northwestern Europe than in Asia.

One important general conclusion should also be drawn. No single condition accounts for the origins of capitalism everywhere. Rather, a number of factors must prevail in order to give birth to capitalism, and it is the

inherited. Joint stock companies did not exist in the Asian countries, but in some cases there were functional equivalents, for example the lineage-owned enterprises in China, which lasted for many decades, even though the original principals had passed away. In Europe, as Pomeranz (*op. cit.*, p. 4) argues, joint stock companies existed but were little utilized until the nineteen century except for long distance trade and colonization.

interaction of these conditions that results in systemic change. Moreover, capitalism often developed quite differently in the countries in which it first appeared than those in which it appeared later because late developers learned from the mistakes of the pioneers. Nevertheless, in this chapter we have outlined a set of conditions that must be present in all countries before the transition to capitalism can take place.

— ❖ **CHAPTER FOUR** ❖ —

Varieties of Capitalism in Industrialized Nations

The general definition of capitalism presented in Chapter 2 allows us to investigate the origins of capitalism, but it does not take us very far in understanding how current capitalist economic systems operate or perform. We need to distinguish between different types of capitalism, and to do this we must get detailed information on the institutions that channel the production and distribution of goods and services.[1] At this point, most analysts stop and, after clearing away the brush,

---

[1] This study uses the definition of institution proposed by Douglas C. North: "a set of rules, conventions, procedures, and moral and ethical behavioral norms designed to constrain the behavior of individuals." North also notes that "If institutions are the rules of the game, organizations and their entrepreneurs are the players. *Organizations* are made up of groups of individuals bound together by some common purpose to achieve certain objectives ... Organizations include political, economic

arbitrarily pick one or two key institutions with which to identify particular forms of capitalism. Using this type of ad hoc procedure, however, makes it difficult to link the distinguishing criteria with the full range of other economic institutions and organizations that structure the society in question. Although such a procedure is useful for some purposes, a more comprehensive approach is required.

The discussion below focuses on the industrialized OECD nations. I look at forty different institutions to explore how they are related, that is, which are complementary and which are substitutes for each other. This type of analysis can be most conveniently implemented by using a statistical technique called cluster analysis, which is explained below. The final results yield four distinct types of capitalism. In further chapters, we will compare their underlying cultural values, their economic performance, and their capacity to make people happy.

(e.g., firms, trade unions, family farms, cooperatives) social (e.g., churches, clubs, athletic associations) and educational groups (e.g., schools, universities, vocational centers)." See his *Structure and Change in Economic History* (New York: Norton & Co., 1981), 201–2; and "Economic Performance through Time." In Carl K. Eicher and John M. Staatz, eds., *International Agricultural Development*, 3d edition (Baltimore, MD: Johns Hopkins University Press, 1998), 84.

A. Approaches to Classifying Capitalist Economic Systems

In the past two centuries, analysts have usually classified capitalist economic systems either by their level of economic development or by their conformity to certain ideal types. The latter approach focuses on characteristics such as the extent of public expenditures, the organization of the labor market, the share of government ownership of the means of production, the most common structure of enterprises, and so forth. As Richard Grassby has sourly noted, ideal types are "fictive generalizations about the predominant characteristics of a particular society, projected from selected historical facts and intended to serve as a basis for universal analysis."[2]

In contrast, I classify capitalist economic systems in terms of the similarities of their institutional configurations, considering both the institutions governing property relations and the institutions of production and distribution. This means that I search for countries in which similar types of complementary institutions cluster together, taking account of governmental participation in the economy and of forty different economic

---

[2]   Richard Grassby, *The Idea of Capitalism before the Industrial Revolution* (Lanham, MD: Rowman & Littlefield, 1999), p. 2.

Varieties of Capitalism in Industrialized Nations

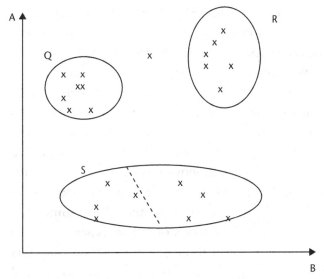

Figure 4–1. *Designation of Clusters*
Note: The axes indicate quantitative measures of institutions. For example axis A could represent the degree to which the economy protects job rights, and axis B, the ratio of government expenditures to GDP. The position of each society is designated by an *x*, and Q, R, and S show the derived clusters.

institutions that structure production, labor, and financial markets. Those nations with similar institutional configurations are then delineated as an economic system. By using this approach we no longer need to rely on one or two arbitrarily selected institutions in the description of the system.

The diagram in Figure 4–1 presents a simplified example of this approach in two dimensions.[3] To be very concrete, let us assume for the moment that the only differences between two economic systems are the degree to which they protect the job rights of workers (represented on axis A) and the ratio of public expenditures to the GDP (represented on axis B). For each of the various nations in the sample, we represent its quantitative scores along these two dimensions with an x. The economies seem to fall into three clusters, whose boundaries are sketched. Those nations in cluster Q have somewhat high job rights and low ratios of public expenditures to the GDP; those in cluster R have relatively high job rights and high ratios of public expenditures to the GDP; and those in cluster C have low job rights and relatively moderate ratios of public expenditures to GDP. The clusters are bunched somewhat differently, with cluster Q being the most tightly packed, and cluster S the most loosely packed. One economy, in the upper-middle portion of the diagram, does not fall clearly into any of the three

[3] Those wishing a more complete discussion of cluster analysis must turn to the technical literature, for example, H. Charles Romesburg, *Cluster Analysis for Researchers* (Belmont CA: Lifelong Learning Publications, 1984). See also Bruce A. Maxwell, Frederic L. Pryor, and Casey Smith, "Cluster Analysis in Cross-Cultural Research," *World Cultures* 13, no. 1 (Spring 2002): 22–39.

clusters; someone else might draw the cluster boundaries to include it in either cluster Q or R. Fortunately, as I have found through experimentation with actual data, such ambiguous situations do not often occur, at least not when delineating economic systems.

The diagram illustrates another problem with this type of analysis: How many clusters should be calculated? Would it be better, for instance, to consider cluster S as two clusters, with the dashed line marking the boundary between them? We face a trade-off. On the one hand, according to the principle of Occam's razor, entities (in this case, the economic systems) should not be multiplied unnecessarily; thus, we should try to end up with as few types of capitalism as possible. On the other hand, increasing the number of clusters reduces the heterogeneity of each cluster, that is, the points will be more closely bunched. In a moment I will derive four clusters of capitalist nations. Several are closely packed, but the *mostly Anglo-Saxon* group of nations is rather heterogeneous and includes Japan, which, in some respects, is quite different from the others. Obviously, if we define twenty-one clusters, each with one society, we will have no error in our description. If, however, six countries (the *x*'s) cluster near each other and another eight are also close to each other but not to the first group, and a third group of seven also forms a distinct cluster, we lose relatively little information about the grouping of nations into distinct economic systems by reducing the twenty-one clusters to three.

In the calculation of the clusters the minimum description length (MDL), a technique devised by Jorma Rissanen, comes in handy.[4] This procedure uses information theory to combine the positive value of the additional information about the properties of the clusters that is gained by increasing their number with the negative value of the greater theoretical complexity that results from the increase of clusters to arrive at a "description length." We can then define the optimal number of clusters as the point where the positive gain in greater descriptive accuracy and the negative value of greater theoretical complexity exactly balance. If we are trying to classify economic systems by their institutional characteristics, the optimal number of clusters is four. The cluster analysis requires no assumptions about the properties of the sample or institutions under examination. However many clusters are chosen, the results are not biased. On the other hand, the results of a cluster analysis

---

4 Jorma Rissanen, *Stochastic Complexity in Statistical Inquiry* (Singapore: World Scientific Publishing Co., 1989), 79ff.; and "Information, Complexity and the MDL Principle." In Lionello F. Punzo, ed., *Cycles, Growth and Structural Change: Theories and Empirical Evidence* (New York: Routledge, 2001), 339–51.

do not speak for themselves; the relative closeness of the elements within a cluster require interpretation. Sometimes, it is also useful to consider clusters that are not optimal. For instance, in the discussion below, I also group countries into five and six clusters in order to determine the homogeneity (and stability) of the individual clusters – which either remain the same or split when more clusters are assumed. The first step is to calculate the description length associated with three, four, five ... ten clusters. Then we select as the optimal number of clusters the one with the smallest description length.[5] The computer program calculating the clusters uses an iterative technique and is run twenty times so as to minimize the possibility that the results of any particular run were influenced by the starting point of the iteration. Once the optimal number of clusters (the number of economic systems) is chosen, the computer program carrying out the tedious delineation of the clusters then prints out the list of economies

[5] In the rare cases, where the MDL is roughly equal for different numbers of clusters, I selected the results yielding the most easily interpretable results. It should be added that in the calculations, all variables are standardized so that their mean is zero and their standard deviation is unity. All institutional elements in the calculation are given equal weight. Using several subsamples of the institutions did not greatly change the results.

in each cluster, as well the properties of each, so that we can gain a clear idea of the institutions that are particularly important in each economic system.

The optimal number of clusters, I must emphasize, may not be very helpful if the derived clusters are very broad. This happens, for example, if the lines defining the clusters in Figure 4–1 encompass such a large area that the nations in a single cluster differ too markedly from each other. The explanatory value of the clustering procedure can be determined by comparing how much the nations in the sample differ from each other without taking the clusters into account with how much the nations within each individual cluster differ from each other.

Although cluster analysis appears objective, it cannot be used heedlessly. Moreover, the number of institutions and organizations that must be taken into account depend on the complexity of the economies involved. For instance, in previous studies of simple hunting and gathering societies, I have used just ten institutions; in studies of agricultural societies, twenty-two institutions; and in this study of OECD nations, forty institutions.[6]

The economic systems derived from the cluster analysis may look at first glance like ideal types, yet they differ in

---

[6] Frederic L. Pryor, "Economic Systems of Foragers," *Cross-Cultural Research* 37, no. 4 (November 2003), 393–426; and "Rethinking

three respects. They are empirically derived, that is, not deduced from a particular theory about economic systems that may or may not be valid. Moreover, the cluster analysis takes into account many different institutions, rather than one or two that capture the investigator's fancy. Finally, in the analysis of ideal types, each society must have all the characteristics of the type, while a cluster analysis allows a more nuanced assessment. That is, a society may lack some of the characteristics that define the system, even though its pattern of institutions and organizations matches the system's characteristics in most important respects.

B. The Economic Systems of OECD Nations in 1990

Cluster analysis can easily be applied to the major industrialized nations of the Organization for Economic Cooperation and Development (OECD). The results, presented below, may not be startling, but they provide a solid basis for the rest of our discussion in this book.

Economic Systems: A Study of Agricultural Societies," *Cross-Cultural Research* 39, no. 3 (August 2005), 252–93.

1. Data and Statistical Technique

The data on forty economic institutions in OECD nations (shown in Table 4–2 and discussed below) draw upon three different types of indicators: Some are derived from the legal specifications of the institutions in question (for instance, various types of government regulation, such as patent protection); others, on statistics about their economic activities (for example, centralization of banks or the percentage of workers covered by collective bargaining contracts); still others, on expert opinion (such as the level of the economy at which wages are most often bargained or the competitiveness of the economic environment).

Of the forty indicators used in the analysis,[7] twelve relate to the market for goods and services, eight to the labor market, six to production and business, seven to governmental activities in the economy, and seven to the financial market. All these indicators reflect what I believe to be crucial aspects of the property, production, and distribution institutions of the economies.

Whenever possible, I collected these indicators for 1990. It is difficult to find more recent data on many institutions; moreover, the Maastricht agreement, signed

---

[7] The detailed description of the indicators and their sources are discussed in Appendix 2 of *Economic Systems of Foraging, Agricultural,*

in 1991, has allegedly accelerated the homogenization of European economic institutions, which would blur the contrast between one nation's economic system and another's. Even so, some institutions specified by the indicators are not related to any specific economic system, which means that the clusters do not explain as much of the differences between economic systems as we might desire.

2. The Overall Results

The MDL approach indicates that the optimal number of clusters for describing the economic systems of the industrialized OECD nations is four. It is, unfortunately, difficult to label them because their constituent institutions cover such a broad field. Nevertheless, since most of the nations in each cluster are geographically close to each other, it is convenient to give them a geographical label, even though it is the institutional configuration, rather than location, that determines which nations are similar to each other. I have also calculated the results assuming five and six clusters in order to gain some idea

and Industrial Societies, available at www.swarthmore.edu/SocSci/Economics/fpryor1.

Table 4–1. *The Derived Economic Systems in the OECD Nations in 1990*

Level of Economic Development (1990 Per Capita GDP)		Level of Economic Development (1990 Per Capita GDP)	
Nordic economic system		*West European economic system*	
Denmark	$18,463	Austria	$16,881
Finland	16,868	Belgium	17,194
Norway	18,470	France (?)	18,083
Sweden	17,680	Germany	18,685
		Netherlands	17,267
South European economic system		*Mostly Anglo-Saxon economic system*	
Greece	9,984	Australia	17,043
Italy	16,320	Canada	18,933
Portugal	10,852	Ireland	11,826
Spain	12,219	Japan	18,789
		New Zealand	13,825
		Switzerland (?)	21,616
		UK	16,411
		USA	23,214

Note: A question mark indicates that the country is on the borderline delineating the cluster. The dollar values are from Angus Maddison (*The World Economy: Historical Statistics* [Paris: OECD, 2003]) and are in the international dollars of 1990 (technically, 1990 Geary-Khamis dollars). The sources of the underlying data on the forty institutions used in this cluster analysis are specified in Appendix 6–2 of *Economic Systems of Foraging, Agricultural, and Industrial Societies* on my web page, www.swarthmore.edu/SocSci/Economics/fpryor1.

about the relative similarity of particular economies within the cluster. Table 4–1 shows the four clusters and their per capita GDP. The *Nordic* economic system is the most homogeneous: the constituent countries are closely grouped, and the composition of this cluster remains constant when the analysis is rerun assuming five and six clusters. By contrast, the *mostly Anglo-Saxon* economic system is the most heterogeneous and the presence of Japan seems anomalous. As expected, the country composition of this group changes somewhat when the analysis is rerun assuming five or six clusters instead of four. Specifically, both Switzerland and Japan lie close to the cluster boundary, so when five clusters are calculated, both hive off. Moreover, when six clusters are calculated, Australia, Ireland, and New Zealand split away from Canada, the United Kingdom, and the United States. The *South European* and *West European* clusters lie relatively close to each other. The *South European* cluster is also relatively stable, although France joins it when five or six clusters are calculated. The *West European* cluster is also relatively stable, except for France, which lies on the border.

Although I interpret the clusters as defining different economic systems, we must ask whether the systems are independent entities or primarily a function of the level of the level of economic development. This problem arises with particular force for a similar cluster analysis of capitalist nations in developing economies.[8] The results from this latter calculation suggest that the systemic differences would disappear as the nations in the sample grow more similar in their level of economic development. Fortunately, for the industrial nations under consideration in this study, this conclusion does not seem valid. Although the *South European* group of nations has a significantly lower average per capita GDP (in 1990 dollars) than those in the other OECD economic systems, the other three clusters are roughly at the same level of economic development. Although we need not at this point determine the direction of causation between the economic system and the level of economic development, I hold the per capita GDP constant (that is, use it as a control variable) at all steps of the later statistical analysis so that its impact on the results is minimized.

The country composition of the four clusters is not surprising, and other economists have come up with roughly the same groupings of nations, using quite different data and statistical techniques.[9] Journalists and

[8]   Frederic L. Pryor, "Economic Systems of Developing Nations," Comparative Economic Studies 48, no. 2 (March 2006): 77–98.

[9]   For instance, Peter A. Hall and David Soskice, eds. *Varieties of Capitalism: The Institutional Foundations of Comparative Advantage*

other observers have also presented similar lists. My results have the advantage that they are derived in a more systematic fashion and, more importantly, use of the cluster technique allows much greater insight into the institutional composition of the economies of the sampled nations.

To view these four capitalist systems from a different standpoint, let us explore the degree of capitalism in each of them using the capitalism scores discussed briefly in Chapter 2. We find that the *mostly Anglo-Saxon* nations score significantly higher on capitalism, and the *South European* nations score significantly lower than the other groups of countries. The *Nordic* and also the *West European* nations lie between these extremes and are not greatly different from each other. These statistical results are also not affected when per capita GDP is held constant. In brief, the different economic institutions in the four types of capitalist systems in the industrial OECD nations partly reflect differences in the degree to which they approximate "pure" capitalism, as defined in Chapter 2. Nevertheless, by dividing the OECD nations into four

(New York: Oxford University Press, 2001); Bruno Amable, *The Diversity of Modern Capitalism* (Oxford: Oxford University Press, 2003); and Jonas Pontusson, *Inequality and Prosperity: Social Europe vs. Liberal America* (Ithaca: Cornell University Press, 2005.

Table 4–2. Defining Characteristics of the Four Industrial Capitalist Economic Systems (Clusters) in 1990

Features		Institutional Indicators	Development Elasticity	Economic Systems			
A	B			Mostly Anglo-Saxon	Nordic	West European	South European
Product market							
1	L	D	Regulation of product market	–	–	–	–	High
2	L	P	Protection of patent rights	+0.66	–	–	–	–
3	L	P	Good legal environment for markets	+0.19	–	–	–	Low
4	LS	PD	Barriers to starting new businesses	–2.21	Low	–	High	High
5	LSX	P	Social partnership of capital and labor	+1.16	Low	High	–	–
6	S	D	Ratio of government subsidies to GDP	–	–	–	–	–
7	S	D	Inter-sectoral grants for R & D	–	–	–	–	–
8	S	D	Foreign trade barriers	–	–	–	–	–
9	XL	D	Freedom to set prices	+0.52	High	–	–	–

10	X	D	Product market competition	—	—	Low	—	—
11	X	D	Effectiveness of antitrust laws	+0.22	High	—	—	—
12	X	PD	Presence of business clusters	—	—	—	—	—
Labor market								
13	S	D	Coverage of collective bargaining agreements	−1.20	Low	—	High	High
14	L	D	Centralization of peak union organizations	—	—	—	—	—
15	L	D	Power of workplace representative	—	—	—	—	—
16	L	D	Legal protection: workers, employment	−0.63	Low	—	—	—
17	L	D	Legal protection: labor bargaining rights	—	—	—	—	High
18	X	D	Coordination of wage negotiations in different industries	—	Low	—	—	—
19	XS	D	Strength of vocational training system	—	Low	High	—	—

(continued)

Table 4-2. (Continued)

Features		Institutional Indicators	Development Elasticity	Economic Systems			
A	B			Mostly Anglo-Saxon	Nordic	West European	South European
20 X	D	Level of economy where wages bargained	–	Low	High	–	–
Production and business sector							
21 S	P	Widespread firm ownership	–	High	–	Low	Low
22 S	P	Importance of large manufacturing firms	+1.26	–	–	–	–
23 L	P	Power of peak organizations	–	Low	High	–	–
24 L	P	Shareholder rights	–	High	–	Low –	Low
25 L	P	Creditor rights	–	–	–	–	–
26 L	P	Significant worker role in firm's decision	–	Low	High	–	–

Government sector

27	S	PD	Govt. direct share of fixed investment	—	—	—	—	—
28	S	D	Govt. share of total consumption	—	—	High	—	—
29	S	D	Ratio of govt. domestic transfers to GDP	—	Low	—	High	—
30	S	P	Govt. direct share of total employment	—	Low	High	High	—
31	S	P	State enterprise share of total employment	—	—	—	—	—
32	S	D	Share of R & D in government sector	−1.66	—	—	—	—
33	L	D	Coverage of social security system	—	—	High	High	—

Financial sector

34	L	D	Central bank independence	+0.99	—	—	High	—
35	L	PD	Restriction on bank activities	—	—	—	—	—
36	L	D	Openness of external capital flow	+3.48	—	—	—	—

(continued)

Table 4–2. *(Continued)*

Features		Institutional Indicators	Development Elasticity	Economic Systems			
A	B			Mostly Anglo-Saxon	Nordic	West European	South European
37	S	PD	Comprehensiveness of accounting standards.	+0.49	–	–	Low	–
38	S	P	Bank concentration	–	–	High	–	Low
39	S	D	Relative size of financial system	+1.01	–	–	–	–
40	S	D	Stock market activity/ bank activity	–	High	–	Low	Low

Notes: The *features* indicate characteristics of the indicators. Column A designates whether the indicator is based on a legal definition (L); a statistic (S); expert evaluations (X); or some combination thereof. Column B designates whether the indicator refers primarily to property relations (P) or production/distribution (D). *Development elasticity* designates the percentage change in the value of the indicator resulting from a 1 percent change in the per capita GDP; values that are not statistically significant are omitted.

The next four columns designate whether the countries with that economic system (excluding two borderline countries, France and Switzerland, as shown in Table 4–1) have a significantly higher value for the indicator than the other countries when the per capita income is removed from consideration. Only results statistically significant at the 0.10 level are presented. The quantitative levels of these relationships determined through a regression analysis can be found in Frederic L. Pryor, *Economic Systems of Foraging, Agricultural, and Industrial Societies* (New York: Cambridge University Press, 2005), pp. 164–5. The sources and exact meaning of each indicator are specified in Appendix 6–2 of this book at www.swarthmore.edu/SocSci/Economics/fpryor1.

distinct economic systems, rather than considering them as points on a continuum of capitalism, we can more easily explore the impact of particular institutions.

3. The Special Characteristics of Each Economic System

Table 4–2 presents data on the forty institutional characteristics used to define the economic systems. To avoid clutter, I present only those results that are statistically significant at the 0.10 level.

The two columns of features describe the general characteristics of each indicator. To clarify the impact of the level of economic development on each indicator, I also present a simple "development elasticity" for each characteristic. This statistic shows by what percentage the indicator will change if the per capita GDP changes by 1 percent. For instance, the degree of protection of patent rights (indicator 2) is significantly and positively related to the level of economic development and increases 0.66 percent for every 1.00 percent change in the per capita GDP. In contrast, the share of research and development (R & D) carried out in the government sector, rather than by industry or universities (indicator 32), is negative, which means it is inversely related to the per capita GDP (the poorer the country, the greater is the share of R & D conducted by the government). Some indicators, such as the ratio of government subsidies to the GDP (indicator 6) have no significant relationship to the per capita GDP.

The next four columns show whether the countries with different types of capitalism are related to a statistically significant (0.10 level) degree to the indicator. Removing the impact of per capita GDP on the results, if the nations with a particular economic system score significantly higher (0.10 level of confidence) than the other nations, a "high" is placed in the column. Similarly, a "low" designates a significantly lower score with the impact of per capita GDP removed.[10] For instance, barriers to starting a new business (indicator 4) are significantly higher in the nations with *South* and *West European* economic systems than in the other nations, while they are significantly lower in the nations with a *mostly Anglo-Saxon* economic system. A glance at the table reveals that

---

[10] More specifically, to determine the relationship between an economic system and a particular institutional indicator, I fitted the data to an equation of the following type: EcSys = a + b DevLev + c I, where EcSys is a variable that is equal to 1 if the society has the specified economic system and equal to 0 if it hasn't; DevLev is the per capita GDP (development level), I is the institutional indicator under examination; and a, b, and c are the calculated coefficients of the formula. For forty indicators and four economic systems, this required 160 calculations. Because the variable to be explained is equal either to 1 or 0, I used a probit regression technique.

the *mostly Anglo-Saxon* and the *Nordic* economic systems are the most different from the others, while the two economic systems found in continental Europe are in most respects relatively similar.

Table 4–2 shows that in the nations with a *mostly Anglo-Saxon* economic system, labor occupies a relatively weak position in comparison with other countries. This means that a smaller share of workers belong to labor unions, workers have less legal protection against job loss and fewer safeguards for collective bargaining, and the system of vocational education is less developed. Workers also have little role in the decision making of their firms and a less apparent social partnership with management than the other nations. In contrast, enterprises enjoy more autonomy than in other nations. Investors face fewer barriers to starting new enterprises; firms have greater freedom to set their own prices; there are fewer national employer organizations to force conformity, and their ownership is spread more widely. Their shareholders receive greater protection of their ownership rights, the firms are more likely to finance their investments through the stock market (rather than banks), and there is less national coordination of wage negotiations of different firms. Finally, their governments have more effective antitrust laws, a smaller share of the total labor force, and a lower ratio of transfer expenditures to the GDP.

The results also show what we already intuitively know, that the nations with a *Nordic* economic system are more centralized in comparison with other nations. Wages are likely to be negotiated not at the firm level, but at the level of the industry or even nationwide; more is invested in training workers, and the social partnership of capital and labor is greater. The market plays a more restricted role. Competition in the product market is less, the role of national employer organizations is relatively strong, and the financial sector is more concentrated. The economic role of the government is also greater. Current government expenditures as a share of GDP are high, the government has a greater share of total employment, and the coverage of the social insurance system is broader.

The nations with a *West European* economic system have a different type of ordered market economy and their characteristics are difficult to summarize. Even when the level of economic development is factored out a higher share of workers in these countries are covered by collective bargaining agreements and they have a high social partnership of labor and capital than in other countries. On the production side, firm ownership is less widespread, rights of minority stockholders are low, accounting standards are less comprehensive, and a smaller share of industrial investment is financed through the stock market. Finally, government transfers as a ratio to the GDP are high, and central bank independence from the government is also high.

Finally, the *South European* economic system represents yet another combination of institutional characteristics. In comparison to other nations in the sample, these countries have more legal protection against job loss, high safeguards for collective bargaining, and a smaller share of workers belonging to labor unions. On the production side, they have more regulation of the product market, a more unfavorable legal environment for markets, more barriers to starting new businesses, fewer stockholder rights, and less concentration of banking activities.

By and large, the results of the cluster analysis should not be greatly surprising to those familiar with the economies of the OECD nations. Nevertheless, it is worth noting that some of the institutional characteristics defining the particular economic systems have been changing over time. For instance, the relatively high ratio of government consumption expenditures to the GDP in the *Nordic* economic system only appeared in the late 1950s. Similarly, since 1990, peak employer organizations in the United States, such as the Business Roundtable, appeared (to some) to be becoming stronger, while in some European nations they were becoming weaker. Chapter 7 deals at greater length with the changes in these economic systems.

Two unexpected findings also deserve notice. Although the government plays an important causal role in many of these institutional indicators, the seven indicators for the size of the government sector turned out to be no more likely to distinguish the economic systems than the other four classes of indicators. This suggests that the traditional focus of economists on the size of the government sector as an exclusive means of categorizing an economic system is misplaced, and that we must pay just as much attention to economic institutions in the other sectors. Similarly, fifteen other indicators, which one might assume would differentiate the various economic systems, do not, in actuality, play this role; rather, they are common characteristics of most advanced capitalist nations.

In brief, this statistical investigation not only illustrates how cluster analysis can be used in economic studies but also confirms in a rigorous fashion what we intuitively "know" about the economic systems of the OECD nations from our general reading.[11] But be aware that although all nations with the same economic system resemble each other in many important respects, each also has its unique features.

[11] At lower levels of economic development, however, the derived economic systems do not lend themselves to such an easy interpretation.

C. Related Features of the Four Types of Economic Systems

1. A Very Long Historical View

Let's take a historical detour to look at economic conditions around the turn of the first millennium. We find that in some striking ways, the conditions prevailing a thousand years ago might have had an influence on the types of capitalism we see in the modern world.

Classifying the types of political authority in medieval agricultural societies, Max Weber distinguished systems that were highly centralized (for instance, *sultanism*) from systems in which political authority and economic power were more dispersed.[12] Among the latter, the most decentralized, he argued, was *feudalism*, where local political leaders inherited authority and were only nominally bound to the center by a formal promise of fealty. In between these extremes was a type of *patrimonialism*, where the ruler tried to forestall the growth of an independent landed aristocracy by awarding benefices only to an office, not to a person or family; such a system was characterized by a pyramid of patron-

---

[12] Max Weber, *The Theory of Social and Economic Organization*, trans. A. M. Henderson and Talcott Parsons (New York: Oxford University Press, 1947 [1922]).

client relations, with the top administrators exercising considerable power. The peasants at the lowest level of the feudal structure were usually serfs, who had very little freedom of movement. In *patrimonialism*, by contrast, peasants had a variety of statuses, depending on the situation; they might have been serfs, landless laborers, or independent peasant farmers.

For many centuries after the turn of the first millennium, *patrimonialism* distinguished the political systems in South Europe (and later in Latin America) from those on the rest of the European continent. The core countries of West Europe, on the other hand, were distinguished by different forms of *feudalism*. In England, *feudalism* was much less embedded in society and featured more individualism, greater personal mobility, a free yeomanry, and more extensive rights of private property (for both men and women), including the free disposal of land.[13] In the Nordic countries, *feudalism* also took a much lighter form, if we can speak of feudalism at all, and historians have explained this in several ways. For instance, Eli Heckscher notes the important role of internal colonization (settling the empty areas) within several of these Nordic countries, a process that emphasized equality

[13] On this issue see Alan Macfarlane, *The Origins of English Individualism* (New York: Cambridge University Press, 1979).

among people rather than dependency on superiors.[14] Moreover, in all these countries (as in England), the long coastal strips in relation to the remaining land mass allowed traders and travelers to avoid road tolls, which provided an easy source of revenue for feudal landlords elsewhere. This placed a brake on feudal expansion. Individual land ownership also seemed to play a more important role in the *Nordic* countries than in *West European* ones. For instance, at the threshold of modern times, the private land holdings of peasants accounted for 96 percent of all agricultural land in Finland, and slightly more than 50 percent in Sweden. I might also add that in these Nordic nations, the social impact of tribes and extended family units lasted far longer than in West Europe, and tended further to discourage feudal tendencies.

Thus the four economic systems of the industrialized OECD nations of Europe today roughly correspond in their geographical distribution to the four major forms of economic organization that prevailed in the same regions a millennium ago, It is certainly tempting to posit a strong causal link between current economic systems

[14] Eli Heckscher, *An Economic History of Sweden*, translated by Gören Ohlin (Cambridge, MA: Harvard University Press, 1963). One section of this book is entitled "The Absence of Feudalism." The datum on land ownership later in the paragraph comes from p. 31.

and these earlier political/economic/social systems, but this would be hard to prove. A variety of other factors have also had an influence on the development of the four economic systems.

2. Geographical/Economic Connections

Mutual influence of countries also plays a role in the determination of the economic systems. OECD nations with the same type of economic system in 1990 in the past usually had stronger geographical/economic connections with each other than they had with other nations at the same time. With the exception of Japan and Switzerland, the *mostly Anglo-Saxon* nations consist exclusively of England and its former colonies or conquered lands. The former colonies drew most of their early European population from the British Isles, founded their legal systems on English principles, and continue to speak English to this day. Similarly, most of the nations with a *West European* economic system were politically united at various times, for instance, during much of the Carolingian period and also under Napoleon. These nations are geographically contiguous, and they have had close political and economic contacts for a millennium. The *Nordic* nations are small and also lie close to each other; for brief periods they also formed political unions for particular purposes. At various times, Sweden and Norway were united, as were Sweden and Finland, and all four *Nordic* nations entered into the Kalmar Union in the late fourteenth century. The legal systems of the four *Nordic* countries stemmed from the same ideas; all four nations have been predominantly Protestant for many centuries; and three of the four speak languages that come from a common root. This closeness is also tempered by the fact that they have also fought each other and occupied each other's lands. The *South European* nations have also had close commercial relations, relying for many centuries on the Mediterranean Sea as their primary transportation linkage, and their current legal systems had the same origins in French civil law. Except for Greece, their languages are similar, and they have been predominantly Roman Catholic. Such geographic/historical factors, which favor diffusion of ideas and institutions, might also provide some explanation of why France, a nation with both strong west and south European contacts, appears close to the boundary between west and south European economic systems.

The Japanese case is more difficult to explain. It moved away from feudalism only in the nineteenth century and, to catch up economically, borrowed ideas heavily from many different nations. This factor, combined with Japan's unique culture, explains why this country is so hard to classify and appears close to the boundary between the *mostly Anglo-Saxon* and *West European* economic systems.

Past disparities in levels of economic development among the four groups of nations have reinforced their divergent systemic tendencies.[15] More specifically, the average per capita GDP of *South European* nations was considerably lower than that of the other three groups of nations by 1700 and has remained so ever since. Because they industrialized later than the *mostly Anglo-Saxon* and the *West European* nations, the average *Nordic* nation also had a somewhat lower per capita GDP, at least until about 1970.

3. Political/Economic Factors

Certain political scientists have argued that the relatively late industrialization of the *Nordic* countries brought about conditions favorable to a distinctive political

[15] I base the generalizations in this paragraph on estimates by Angus Maddison (*The World Economy: Historical Statistics* [Paris: OECD, 2003 For estimates of the average per capita GDP for the *mostly Anglo-Saxon* nations for 1500 and 1700, I omitted Australia, Canada, New Zealand, and the United States, because they were being colonized in this period and had substantial native populations; and I also omitted New Zealand in 1820 for the same reason. For 1870, however, I used the full sample (excluding France and Switzerland because of the ambiguous designation of their economic systems).

coalition between agricultural and industrial workers, one that had a considerable impact on the development of the welfare states in these countries.[16] Among the *South European* nations, three – Italy, Portugal, and Spain – went through long periods in which the government pursued certain policies of centralized corporatism. These eras of centralization influenced certain economic institutions in later years, at least up to the end of the twentieth century. Similarly, in the aftermath of World War II, the nations that now have the *West European* economic system engaged in considerable nationalization of industry and, moreover, adopted certain institutions of decentralized corporatism.[17] Although these countries later reversed many of these changes, they play a role in explaining certain unique aspects of their economic systems.

While it is satisfying to find some deep-rooted historical, geographical, and political factors underlying the four types of capitalism found in the OECD nations in

---

[16] James Kurth, "A Tale of Four Countries: Parallel Politics in South Europe, 1815–1990." In James Kurth and James Petras, eds., *Mediterranean Paradoxes: Politics and Social Structure in Southern Europe* (Providence, RI: Berg, 1993), 27–66.

[17] These changes are described in Frederic L. Pryor, "Corporatism as an Economic System," *Journal of Comparative Economics* 12, no. 3, 1988.

1990, I must add the precautionary note: random factors, such as war, depressions, and government policy have had in some cases important influences on the economic system as well. Let us digress for a moment to glance at Italy and Japan and show how such random factors can also shape the system.

Although Italy and Japan had quite different histories, both were poor when they started to industrialize in the last decades of the nineteenth century. Both began with the same model for the administration of enterprises, namely, a pyramidal system of holding companies whereby a small group – often a family – would control a vast number of enterprises, with little interference from stockholders at lower levels of the pyramid. Both nations also had an extraordinarily large number of small and medium-sized enterprises and both had relatively underdeveloped banking systems.

Nevertheless, subsequent events caused their economic systems to diverge greatly. In Italy, many of the companies suffered financial difficulties in the 1930s and were nationalized, thus creating several very large government holding companies that lasted for many decades. Italy also never developed an extensive banking system, so that the government served as a key lender to private enterprises. In Japan, by way of contrast, the large conglomerates (*zaibatsu*) created banks to serve their own financial needs, and these large banks survived and prospered for many decades. Although the American occupation of Japan after World War II led to the partial dismantling of the *zaibatsu*, their core banks still remained, and large enterprises still continued to flourish.

Although the governments of both nations attempted to implement various industrial policies, Japan's strategy was more consistently and skillfully carried out; and, as a result, large enterprises benefited much more from government incentives than those in Italy did. The Japanese government's economic policies also had a particularly strong impact on the structure of exports. After World War II, Japan's exports shifted from steel and ships in the 1950s to cars and low-tech electronics in the next two decades, and to more knowledge-intensive goods thereafter, all produced primarily by large firms and encouraged by government agencies. In Italy the commodity composition of exports has not changed so greatly and continues to be dominated by more traditional manufactured goods, produced by small and middle-size enterprises.

Many other differences could be mentioned. The main point is that the economies of these two latecomers to industrialization diverged considerably from each other in the last century, primarily because of a series of incremental changes, influenced in large measure by strong forces, particularly of a political nature, from outside the economic system.

D. Review and Preview

The technique of cluster analysis, applied to data for the major economic institutions of the OECD nations, permits us to distinguish four distinct types of capitalism and to define them more rigorously than before. Countries with the same system show a similar configuration of their product and labor markets, in production and business, in certain economic roles of government, and in the financial sector. In the past these countries also shared many similar institutional characteristics as well, have had relatively similar levels of economic development, and have had considerable political and social interchange.

Now that we have isolated these four economic systems, we face two immediate tasks. The first is to explore the influence of a nation's culture on its economic system, which is undertaken in the next chapter. The second is to investigate the impact of these systems on their economic and social performance, a task for Chapters 6 and 7, which also delve into the question of whether the level of performance is due to the system itself, to particular groups of institutions, or to single institutions and whether policy decisions, exogenous events, or random factors also play important roles.

— ❖ CHAPTER FIVE ❖ —

Cultural Influences on the Economic System

E conomic systems do not stand alone: they are influenced by, and have an impact on, other aspects of
society. Although economists often pay attention to
political factors, they usually take little notice of culture. This chapter attempts to correct that oversight.

As we saw in Chapter 3, the cultural characteristics
of a nation do not tell us anything about its *degree* of
capitalism. Nevertheless, in this chapter I show that culture has a strong correlation with the *type* of capitalism.
Of course, correlation does not mean causality, but by
comparing the cultural and economic systems of communist East Germany and capitalist West Germany, we
will see that in democratic nations, culture influences
the economic system more strongly than the economic
system influences culture. On the other hand, in non-
democratic nations this generalization does not necessarily hold.

Cultural Influences on the Economic System

The first step is to delineate cultural systems and to show a strong parallelism between cultural and economic systems. Then I examine some aspects of change in cultural systems over time and explore how the experience of the two Germanies yields insights into the direction of causality between the economic and cultural systems.

A. Cultural Systems: The Basic Approach

The concept of culture is vague and protean. A. L. Kroeber and Clyde Kluckholm found over 150 definitions of culture in the literature of the social sciences and argued that the many definitions emphasize quite different characteristics, ranging from artifacts and material traits to social structures and behaviors, beliefs, psychological orientations, symbols, and values and norms.[1] I use the concept of culture to refer to the shared values, beliefs, attitudes, and social/personal orientations of the population that might have some relevance to economic activity (but are not directly related to the institutions defining the economic system).

[1] Albert L. Kroeber and Clyde Kluckholm, "Culture: A Critical Review of Concepts and Definitions," *Papers of the Peabody Museum of American Archeology and Ethnology, Harvard University*, no. 47 (Cambridge, MA: Peabody Museum, 1952).

For data on culture we turn to the World Values Survey, a standardized international public opinion survey, and select for 1990–93, the years corresponding to the delineation of the economic systems in the previous chapter.[2] This source serves our purposes well: the samples for each country are quite large (all over a thousand people) and are weighted to reflect the general population; the questions posed to the respondents cover a wide variety of cultural characteristics; and similar surveys are also available for 1980 and 2001, so that we can explore how these characteristics change over a two-decade period.

To determine which questions from the World Values Survey to select, I first cluster-analyzed the entire set of 222 reported values and determined that the optimal number of clusters was five. To obtain a more manageable sample, I selected forty-one values, listed in Table 5–2, which had the greatest relevance to economic activity. Then I carried out another cluster analysis on this smaller sample to isolate five clusters (using the MDL approach) and to determine the countries included in each cluster.[3] The country composition of the five

[2] Ronald Inglehart, Miquel Basáñez, and Alejandro Moreno, *Human Values and Beliefs* (Ann Arbor, MI: University of Michigan Press, 1998).

[3] I discuss the technical aspects of my methods in Frederic L. Pryor, "Cultural and Economic Systems," *American Journal of Economics*

clusters from the smaller sample was quite similar to that of the larger sample. The five clusters determined which countries had the most similar configuration of values and attitudes, a configuration I define as the cultural system.

B. The Congruence of Economic and Cultural Systems

Table 5–1 presents the five cultural systems derived for the OECD nations; lined up with their corresponding economic systems. (For easy comparisons, I recalculated the economic systems of the OECD countries into five clusters, rather than four.) Although the cultural systems are defined in terms of values, the labels of these systems also refer to the geographical area in which the most of the countries are located. The key result can be

and Sociology 66, no. 4 (October 2007): 817–55. Although in many cases cultural systems shape economic systems, the direction of causality can run the other way. For instance, the answer to a question about interpersonal trust reflects both a person's basic values and, to a certain extent, the impact of the economic system on interpersonal relations. For this reason, we might expect a certain correlation between economic system and values. I have tried, however, to select those questions from the World Values Survey in which this problem of reverse causality, while not eliminated, does not appear to be highly probable.

Table 5–1. *Cultural and Economic Systems of OECD Nations in 1990*

Cultural Systems (C)	Economic Systems (E)
Mostly Anglo-Saxon (MAS-C)	*Mostly Anglo-Saxon (MAS-E)*
Canada	Canada
Ireland	Ireland
U.K.	U.K.
U.S.	U.S.(?)
	Australia
	New Zealand
Switzerland	
Nordic (NO-C)	*Nordic (NO-E)*
Denmark	Denmark
Norway	Norway
Sweden	Sweden
	Finland
West European (WE-C)	*West European (WE-E)*
Austria	Austria
Netherlands	Netherlands
West Germany	West Germany
	Belgium
	Switzerland (?)
Finland	
South European (SE-C)	*South European (SE-E)*
France	France
Italy	Italy
Portugal	Portugal
Spain	Spain
	Greece
Belgium	
Other(O-C)	*Other(O-E)*
Japan	Japan

Note: Australia, New Zealand, and Greece are not included in the World Value Study. The economic systems are somewhat different from those listed in Table 4–1 because five clusters, rather than four, are calculated. Since Switzerland has data for only about half of the cultural characteristics, its placement was determined by means of a supervised-cluster technique after the five clusters were determined without it. A question mark indicates that the country is on the border of the cluster.

easily summarized: the country composition of the five clusters designating the economic and cultural systems is relatively similar. More specifically, of the countries in the seventeen-country sample, 88 percent fall in the parallel economic and cultural systems; if Switzerland is added to the sample, this score falls to 83 percent. In both cases this congruence is statistically significant at the 0.01 level.[4]

Before turning to the question of causality, however, it is worthwhile briefly to explore the distinguishing characteristics of these various cultural systems. Table 5–2 gives brief descriptions of each of the values included in the cluster analysis. As in Table 4–2, for each indicator I tested whether the score for the countries with a given cultural system was significantly (.10 level) higher (designated by "high" in the table) or lower (designated "low") than the other countries, holding the level of per capita GDP constant.

The conventional wisdom holds that the nations in the *mostly Anglo-Saxon* cultural cluster have more individualistic cultural characteristics, and in some respects this seems to be true. People living in these nations are more

---

[4] This parallelism between economic and cultural systems may not be universal. It appears to break down, for instance, in the case of capitalist (or proto-capitalist) countries at very low levels of economic development.

Table 5-2. Indicators Used to Derive the Cultural Systems

WVS Variable Number	Cultural Characteristic	Cultural Systems				
		Mostly Anglo-Saxon-C	Nordic-C	West Europe-C	South Europe-C	Japan-C
General orientation toward life						
V70, 76–7, 81	Don't want neighbors who are Muslims, Jews, foreigners, those of another race.	Low	–	–	High	High
V94	Believe that generally speaking, people can be trusted.	–	High	–	Low	–
V95	Believe that we have freedom of choice, control over our lives.	–	–	–	–	Low
V97b	Believe people live in economic need because they are lazy, lack will power.	High	Low	–	–	–
V127a	Believe one should follow boss's instruction and not wait to be convinced.	High	–	Low	–	–
V135	Believe life is meaningful only because God exists.	High	Low	–	–	–

V141	Believe there are clear guidelines about what is good and evil	High	Low	–	–	–
V224	Believe one should love parents regardless of their faults.	–	–	–	–	–
V225	Believe parents should do best for children, even at their own expense.	–	–	Low	High	Low
V227	Believe important for parents to encourage children to be independent.	–	High	–	Low	–
V228	Believe important for parents to encourage children to work hard.	–	Low	Low	High	–
V229	Believe important for parents to encourage children to feel responsible.	Low	High	–	–	–
V230	Believe important for parents to encourage children's imagination.	–	–	–	–	–
V233	Believe important for parents to encourage children to have determination	–	–	–	–	High

(Continued)

Table 5–2. *(Continued)*

WVS Variable Number	Cultural Characteristic	Cultural Systems				
		Mostly Anglo-Saxon-C	Nordic-C	West Europe-C	South Europe-C	Japan-C
V235	Believe important for parents to encourage children to be unselfish.	High	–	Low	–	–
V264	Believe less emphasis should be placed on money and material possessions.	–	–	–	–	–
V265	Believe less importance should be placed on work in our lives.	–	–	–	–	–
V324	Believe new ideas are generally better than old ideas.	High	–	–	–	Low
Political/social beliefs						
V10	Occasionally or frequently discuss politics with friends.	–	High	High	Low	–
V16	Would trade off employment reduction for environmental improvement.	–	–	Low	High	–

V129	Believe when jobs are scarce, people should be forced to retire early.	—	—	High	Low
V131	Believe if able bodied can't find jobs, unfair to give jobs to handicapped.	—	—	—	High	—
V250	Believe there should be given greater incentives for individual effort.	—	—	—	Low	—
V251	Believe government ownership of business and industry should be increased.	—	—	Low	High	—
V252	Believe state should be more responsible so that all are provided for.	—	—	—	—	High
V253	Believe unemployed should have right to refuse a job offer.	High	—	—	—	—
V254	Believe competition is harmful and brings out the worst in people.	—	Low	Low	Low	High	—
V256	Believe wealth can grow so enough for everyone.	—	—	High	—	—

(Continued)

Table 5-2. (Continued)

WVS Variable Number	Cultural Characteristic	Cultural Systems				
		Mostly Anglo-Saxon-C	Nordic-C	West Europe-C	South Europe-C	Japan-C
V259a	Believe most important goal for government is maintaining order.	—	High	—	—	—
V268	Believe greater respect should be given to those in authority.	High	Low	—	—	Low
V298	Believe cheating on taxes cannot be justified.	—	—	—	—	High
V275, V278–80	Have confidence in country's legal system, police, parliament, civil service	—	High	—	Low	—
V282	Have confidence in Social Security system.	—	—	High	—	—
V308	Believe prostitution is never justified.	—	—	Low	—	—

Beliefs about personal life

V87 .	During the past few weeks, have you felt lonely, remote from others.	—	—	High	—	—	—
V103 .	Believe important that my job have good promotion prospects.	High	—	—	—	—	—
V110	Believe important for my job to allow achievement.	High	—	—	—	—	—
V112	Believe important for my job to be interesting.	High	—	—	—	Low	Low
V116	Believe my job is satisfying	—	—	—	—	Low	—
V117	Believe my job allows a great deal of freedom to make decisions.	—	—	—	—	—	—
V330	Believe I own many things others envy me for.	—	—	High	—	—	—

Note: WVS = World Values Survey. The country composition of the economic systems is specified in Table 5–1. "High" and "low" designate whether the values of the countries with the particular economic system are significantly (0.10 level) higher or lower than those of the other OECD nations when the GDP per capita is held constant. Results that are not significantly different are not noted.

likely to believe that people live in poverty because they are lazy and lack will power (V97b). By contrast, they are more tolerant of those who are unlike themselves (V70). Unexpectedly, they are more likely to believe that greater respect (than currently) should be given to those in authority (V268) and that they should follow their boss's instructions without question, even if they disagree with them (V127a). They are more likely to believe that children should be taught to be unselfish and less likely to believe that they should be taught to be responsible. Finally, they have significantly higher belief in God and in the existence of clear guidelines about what is good and evil.

Those living in the *Nordic* nations show significantly more interpersonal trust (V94), greater confidence in their political institutions (V275), and greater desire for maintenance of law and order (V259a). At the same time, they are more likely to believe in the importance of teaching children to be independent (V227) and responsible (V229), but less likely to believe that they should be taught to work hard (V228). Finally, they are more likely to discuss politics with their friends (V10). Such results also do not correspond to popular views of "socialistic" Scandinavians.

In many respects, those living in the *West European* nations correspond to misguided stereotypes about "left-wing" people. They reveal feelings of significantly greater alienation (V87) and envy (V330) than those in other cultural systems. They are less inclined to believe that children should be taught to be unselfish (V235) and less likely to stress that children should be encouraged to work hard (V228). They are also less willing to trade lower unemployment rates for a worsening of the environment (V16). They are more likely to believe that wealth can grow so that there is enough for everyone (V256). They are significantly less likely to believe that government ownership should increase (V251).

Those living in the *South European* nations are significantly less likely than those in other countries to trust others (V94) or their government (V275). If a choice must be made, they are more likely to place importance on reducing unemployment than on combating environmental degradation (V16) and are less likely to believe that the handicapped should be given work when able-bodied people are unemployed (V131). They believe more than those in other cultural systems that children should be taught to work hard (V228) and less that children should be encouraged to be independent (V227). They are more likely to believe that competition is harmful and brings out the worst in people.

Finally, the *Japanese* (the only nation in the "other" cluster) are significantly less likely than people in other nations to believe that we have control over our lives (V95) and that new ideas are generally better than old ones (V324). They tend more to believe that children should be taught to have determination (V233) and less that one's job should be interesting (V112). Contrary to the conventional wisdom about the Japanese, they are *less* likely to believe that more respect should be given to those in authority (V268). At the same time, they are more likely to believe that the state should take more responsibility to see that all are provided for (V252).

While these individual cultural characteristics have a certain interest, in almost all cases their links with a particular type of economic system are very indirect.[5] Moreover, no single cultural characteristic alone appears to define the distinguishing features of a particular economic system and the patterns of individual characteristics do not reveal a simple interpretation. That is, it is difficult to characterize these cultural systems in any

---

[5] This was tested using the following type of logit regression for the 17-country sample for the individual cultural characteristics: $ES_c = a + b\ CC_c$, where ES is a zero-one variable indicating one of the economic systems, CC is a single cultural characteristic, and the subscript c indicates a country. Very few of these regressions yielded a statistically significant b coefficient. The results were not meaningfully changed when per capita GDP of the various countries was added to the regression.

sweeping way, an uncomfortable conclusion for those who like facile explanations. For the rest of this discussion, however, I focus only on the systems and not their individual components.

C. Causal Relationships between Cultural and Economic Systems

To explore causal links between cultural and economic systems, we first need to determine the stability of the cultural systems. In Chapter 8 I show that economic systems change slowly. If cultural systems change rapidly, then the correlation between the two systems in 1990 is fortuitous. If the stability of the cultural systems can be established, we can then turn quickly to the issues about causation.

1. Stability of the Cultural System

Stability has two aspects: Over time, do we find the same countries still clustering together, even though their individual characteristics may be changing? And (an even stronger manifestation of stability), do the values of the individual cultural characteristics remain roughly the same over time? The results shown below show that cultural systems do not appear to change quickly in a manner that would have much impact on the economic system.

a. Changing Composition of Countries with a Given Cultural System. The only comparable data on cultural values for the OECD nations in 1990–93 are surveys for 1981 and for 1999–2002 that each ask twenty-five similar questions.[6] The surveys for 1981 and 1990–93 contain nine countries that are the same; the surveys for 1990–93 and 1999–2002 cover eighteen countries that are the same (and ask thirty-two questions that are similar in both surveys).

Various comparisons show that the country composition of the clusters remains quite similar over time. More specifically, in the sample of twenty-five characteristics, 89 percent of the nine countries in 1981 are clustered together in 1990–93; further, 78 percent are in the same clusters in 1999–2002. For the larger group of thirty-two characteristics, 85 percent of the eighteen nations that

---

[6] These three surveys are the European Values Survey of 1981 (UK Data Archive, *European Values Survey: User Notes* http://www. data-archiv.ac.uk9 (accessed 2005) and the World Values Surveys of 1990–93 (Inglehart, et al., *op. cit.* [1998]), and of 1999–2002 (Ronald Inglehart, Miguel Basáñez, Jaime Díez-Medrano, Loek Halman, and Ruud Luijkx, *Human Beliefs and Values* [Mexico City: Siglo XXI Editores, 2004]).

were clustered together in 1990–93 are in the same clusters in 1999–2002. Moreover, in all cases, the country composition of these various clusters is very similar to that shown in Table 5–1.

b. Changes in Individual Cultural Characteristics. Between 1981 and 1990–93, the numerical values of the twenty-five individual characteristics that define the cultural systems for the nine-nation sample changed, on average, 20 percent; between 1990–93 and 1999–2002, they changed 10 percent, and between 1981 and 1999–2002, 24 percent.[7] Given the relative stability of the country composition of the cultural systems, these changes over time in the individual value, although apparently large, may only represent random variations due to errors in sampling. Alternatively, they may also represent the impact of changing per capita GDP, age distributions, and other causal variables. The discussion below does not require a resolution of this difficult issue. Nevertheless, it must be emphasized that, to the extent to which cultural systems as a whole experienced change, the individual characteristics within the same cultural

---

[7] Since the survey data present the percentage of people agreeing with the various statements, the results presented in terms of percentage point changes are considerably less.

system changed to the same magnitude, so that the clusters retained their country composition over time.

2. Causal Links between Cultural and Economic Systems

Does the economic system shape culture? Or is it the other way around? Social scientists of different stripes clash vigorously on this issue. Many Marxists would have us believe that the economic system is the basic variable and that cultural characteristics are merely "superstructure," determined by the base. Others argue the reverse: in a democracy the cultural system is the key variable, and it in large measure determines the economic system; if this were not the case, the government, which has a strong impact on the economic system, would be voted out of office. A third position, justified both on theoretical grounds and anecdotally, is that cultural characteristics and systems evolve together, which means that, over time, the cultural and economic systems should change at roughly the same pace.[8]

---

[8] This position is argued by Robert Sugden, "Normative Expectations: The Simultaneous Evolution of Institutions and Norms." In Avner Ben-Nur and Louis Putterman, eds., *Economics, Values, and Organization* (New York: Cambridge University Press, 1998), 73–100.

Cultural Influences on the Economic System

Even for the OECD countries, it is hard to investigate the issue quantitatively because the lack of suitable data over long periods of time prevents the use of certain standard statistical techniques. Fortunately, we can take advantage of a natural experiment occurring in East and West Germany, where each country adopted quite different economic and political systems after World War II. Although a case study of two nations does not definitively resolve the issue of causation, it can provide some important insights.

At the end of World War II in 1945, the living standards, the economic structure, and the economic systems of the two parts of Germany were roughly the same. In the preceding three- quarters of a century these two parts of Germany had the same central government and the same political parties, and for many centuries before that, of course, the same language and literature. Thus it seems highly likely that the cultural systems in East and West Germany were roughly similar as well at the end of the war.[9] I will show below that, by the time the Berlin Wall fell forty-four years later, they still had

[9] It should be remembered that the current "East" Germany corresponds to the former "central" Germany of the prewar period. The evidence for these generalizations about the economy comes from Wolfgang Stolper, *The Structure of the East German Economy* (Cambridge, MA: Harvard University Press, 1960), 3, 441.

roughly similar cultural characteristics, even though their economic systems had grown vastly different in the interim.[10]

In East Germany, the general population had very little influence on the choice of their leaders or on how the economy was organized. Rather, a dictatorship of the Communist Party, following the general guidelines for economic management provided by the USSR, forced a new economic system onto its population. In West Germany, the government was democratically elected, the economic system represented an evolution from the interwar arrangements, and the government was much

---

[10] Of course, other countries were also split after the end of World War II. In "National Values and Economic Growth." *American Journal of Economic and Sociology* 64, no. 2 (2005): 451–85, I present evidence that, like East and West Germany, cultural values in China and Taiwan in the early 1990s were surprisingly similar. Unfortunately, this is not a clean experiment since, at the end of World War II, the ethnic composition of the two nations has been somewhat different. Another useful comparison about the impact of communist and market economies might be North and South Vietnam, but unfortunately the requisite data are not available. The same difficulty arises for comparing values in North and South Korea, but in this case I would guess that the values in these two countries would not be similar, given the extreme measures taken by the North Korean government to change the mentality of the population and the difficulties North Korean refugees have had in adjusting to life in South Korea.

more constrained by the values and demands of its citizens in its decisions about shaping the institutions that made up its economic system.

If economic systems determined cultural systems, then the cultural systems of the two Germanies should have been greatly different in the fall of 1990, a year after the fall of the Berlin Wall, when the World Values Survey was carried out in the two parts of Germany. If the cultural systems of the two Germanies remained relatively similar after forty-four years during which their economic systems had radically diverged, it suggests that the economic system has little impact on values and that the reverse line of causation is more likely, at least in cases where the population can influence the economic system.

As a first step toward disentangling these issues, I start with forty-one questions from the World Values Survey and compare East German cultural characteristics with those of Russia, of three nearby East European countries (Czechoslovakia, Slovenia, and Poland), of the countries in the *West-European*-C cluster, excluding West Germany (namely, Austria, the Netherlands, and Finland),[11] and finally, of West Germany alone.

---

[11] This is a highly technical note. Using the entire seventeen-nation sample for 1990, I carried out a supervised-cluster analysis to

The results of such a comparison show that East German values resembled most closely those of West Germany; in turn, the next closest group of countries was the *West European*-C cluster (excluding West Germany); and these were then followed by the three nearby East European countries. Values in Russia were the most different from those in East Germany. Repeating the same process with 186 other values that were not so directly related to economic activities yielded the same results. The cultural similarity between the Germanies can be concretely seen in the answers to particular questions in the World Values Survey. For instance, West and East Germans placed much more value on job security and less value in teaching their children to be unselfish than did people in the average West European nation.

But even though the values of East Germany resembled those of West Germany more than they resembled to those of other nations, the average scores in the two parts of Germany differed by 21 percent. This difference

determine which of the five cultural systems in the OECD nations East Germany most closely resembled. Two different techniques for carrying out such an analysis (a k-nearest neighbor and an archetype average) both showed that the East German cultural characteristics most closely resembled those of the group (cluster) of countries that included West Germany.

is roughly the same as the average change in the value scores over a decade, as shown above. This issue requires further investigation, especially to determine the extent to which this difference was a function of the level of economic development. The two parts of Germany had quite different average income levels in 1990.

Using all the nations in the sample to calculate the relationship between level of economic development and the scores for each value, one can determine what the West German value scores would have been if its per capita GDP had been the same as East Germany's.[12] Then I compared this result with the actual East German results. The predicted and actual values for East Germany were found on average to differ only between 8 and 12 percent, results that lie well within the random deviations of the cultural characteristics at two different points in

---

[12] This is another technical note. For this analysis I employed a three-step procedure: First I calculated a regression with the seventeen market economies for each value characteristic, using as explanatory variables per capita income and a dummy variable for West Germany. Other variables could have been added to the regression that might have a small impact on the cultural characteristics, for instance, the distribution of the labor force in different industrial branches. Nevertheless, the small amount of added explanatory value of such a step did not seem to outbalance the loss of valuable degrees of freedom. Then from these regressions

time (see above, section C-1-b). In brief, although the East German cultural characteristics varied in certain respects from those of West Germany, the impact of the East German economic system did not seem to directly account for much cultural divergence.

A strange corroboration of this conclusion occurred during my interview with an extremely high official of the former SED (Sozialistische Einheitspartei Deutschlands, that is, the Communist Party) in East Berlin in April 1990. When asked about the recent East German election results, which favored the Christian Democrats, he lamented: "We had forty years to change the mentality of our people – and we failed."

In brief, the economic system of East Germany during its communist period does not appear to have had a strong impact on its overall cultural system except in so far as it held back the economic growth of that country. Another possible shard of evidence for the potential primacy of cultural over economic characteristics is provided by Joachim Zweynert and Nils Goldschmidt, who note that in the transition to capitalism in East and Central Europe, one group of nations (Poland, Hungary,

---

I determined what West Germany's values would have been if its per capita GDP had been the same as East Germany's. Finally, I compared this result with actual East German results.

the Czech Republic, Slovakia, Slovenia, Croatia, and the Baltic States) has been much more successful and consistent in their implementation of Westernizing reforms than a second group has been (Russia, Belarus, Bulgaria, Moldavia, the Ukraine, and Romania).[13] All countries in the first group practice a predominantly Western version of Christianity (Roman Catholicism and Protestantism), while different versions of Eastern Orthodoxy prevail in the countries of the second group. Zweynert and Goldschmidt argue that accompanying these two distinct versions of Christianity are two quite different sets of values, views of life, and traditions, using as an example the divergent views on the proper boundaries (or lack thereof) between the political, civic, economic, and religious realms. This is a tantalizing and reasonable hypothesis, but it is difficult to prove conclusively.

3. Interpretation of the Evidence

This analysis does not claim that the direction of causation between the economy or the economic system and the cultural system goes *only* in one direction. In

---

[13] Joachim Zweynert and Nils Goldschmidt, "The Two Transitions in Central and Eastern Europe as Processes of Institutional Transplantation, "*Journal of Economic Issues* 40, no. 4 (2006): 895–918.

advanced societies, as noted above in the case of trust, (note 3 in this chapter), the economic system can structure values, and the influence of the economic system on other cultural characteristics also seems likely. Nor do I claim that the causal priority of the cultural over the economic system is universal and divorced from historical circumstances.[14] Nevertheless, the comparison between East and West Germany tentatively suggests that in democratic nations, the direction of causation is *primarily* from cultural values to economic system, a conclusion that is also consistent with the parallelism between cultural and economic systems.

Influencing both the cultural and the economic systems are a variety of broader causal factors. The most important of these is probably the level of economic development. Since the OECD countries studied here (except for the four *South European* nations) have roughly the same level of economic development, it seems unlikely that this factor accounts for the congruence between the economic and cultural systems shown in Table 5–1. Some microeconomic factors can also explain some of the correlation between some cultural and

[14] This relationship does not hold for very poor capitalist nations. See Frederic L. Pryor, "Economic Systems of Developing Nations," *Comparative Economic Studies* 48, no. 1 (2006): 77–98.

economic characteristics. For instance, certain governmental transfer programs may, over time, induce a sense of entitlement so that, in this sense, the economic system creates change in the cultural system.[15] In interpreting the results of this comparison of West and East Germany, one last consideration must be taken into account. The cultural characteristics that are most influenced by the level of economic development would, in all probability, also be most influenced by other characteristics of the economy or the economic system as well. Therefore, if per capita GDP does have an impact on cultural characteristics, it would be on political/social

---

[15] Some of these effects are discussed by Samuel Bowles in "Endogenous Preferences: The Cultural Consequences of Markets and Other Economic Institutions," *Journal of Economic Literature* 36, no. 2 (1998): 75–111. He brings forward many examples, both from real life and experimental games, where the economic institutions have a considerable impact on the cultural characteristics of the situation and the choices made by individuals. He also specifies a number of interesting self-reinforcing mechanisms tying cultural characteristics to particular economic characteristics. Along these lines, an individual's position in the economy also has an important impact on his or her values and actions, irrespective of the average cultural characteristics of the country as a whole. A different set of issues on the relation of the economic system and values is raised in John Templeton Foundation, ed., *Does the Free Market Corrode Moral Character?* (West Conshohocken, PA: Templeton, 2008).

beliefs, rather than on one's views toward oneself or one's general orientation toward life.

The results of a statistical investigation of these ideas are illuminating. When the cultural system is held constant in a regression calculation, we find that per capita GDP has a significant impact on six of the sixteen political/social characteristics specified in Table 5–2. These include discussing politics with friends (V10), willingness to trade off reduction of unemployment for environmental improvement (V16), believing that people should be forced to retire early when jobs are scarce (V129), believing that government ownership should be increased (V251), believing that the state should take more responsibility to see that all are provided for (V252), and believing that competition is harmful and brings out the worst in people (V254). On the other hand, similar calculations show that per capita GDP has no significant impact on the sixteen orientation characteristics specified in Table 5–2 and that it has a significant impact on only two of the seven characteristics relating to the beliefs about personal life.

These results suggest two important conclusions. Even though the cultural system has a critical influence on determining the economic system as a whole, the commonsense argument that the economic system influences some cultural characteristics is also confirmed.

Furthermore, the conjecture that direct political/social beliefs are likely to be the most strongly affected by the economic system also receives support.

D. Some Open Questions

The analysis up to now raises a number of important but unanswered questions that require much more analysis than present space limitations permit. They have been the focus of a large literature associated in the nineteenth century with such names as Karl Marx, or in the twentieth century with Max Weber, Albert Hirschman, or Eric Mielants. For instance, if the cultural system is the main determinant of the economic system, what causes the cultural system to change? In some cases the answer is clear: singular events that cause a nation to reexamine its values and change its institutions accordingly. Such special events include a military defeat, economic depressions, massive immigration or emigration, or a shift in the dominant religion. For instance, within a decade after the Crimean War, Russians reconsidered many of their values and introduced significant changes to its economic system, including the abolition of serfdom. After World War II, Japan also experienced a change in values and made many important changes in its economic system, albeit under the direction of Douglas McArthur and the U.S. occupation forces (changes which have persisted ever since). Some have taken this argument one step further and present evidence that even if a war is successful, it changes a population's beliefs about the proper role of government in the subsequent years, though other values may not be affected.[16] Examples of religious changes that transformed culture, and later the economy include the Protestant Reformation.

However, a nation's values usually change slowly, not in sudden bursts, and such changes and their impact on the economic system are much more difficult to analyze. For instance, the economic system of the United Kingdom moved from a relatively regulated economy of the *West European* type to a relatively liberal economy of the *mainly Anglo-Saxon* type over the course of the latter half of the twentieth century. Linking this systemic transformation to cultural changes during this period requires time-series data on cultural characteristics, and such data are difficult to find. But assuming we could find them, we would then be in a position to test three competing explanations about this change in the U.K.'s

---

[16] Alan T. Peacock and Jack Wiseman, *The Growth of Public Expenditures in the United Kingdom* (Princeton, NJ: Princeton University Press, 1961).

economic system: (1) It was merely a delayed dismantling of the wartime measures and did not reflect real
changes in the values of the population; (2) the change
in the economic system was preceded by a major shift in
values (which would provide further evidence to support
my view about the causal predominance of culture over
the economic system); or (3) it was primarily a pragmatic
response to the weak performance of the economic system in the immediate postwar years and had nothing to
do with deeper cultural values. This case is discussed in
greater detail in Chapter 8.

Another open question concerns the mechanisms by
which the cultural system influences the economic system. In certain cases a "founder effect" is evident, that
is, institutions are established according to the values
of those who established them or who set the policies
that led to their establishment. The political system of
the United States today is still greatly influenced by the
men who attended the Constitutional Convention in
Philadelphia in 1787. In other cases, the cultural characteristics of the society influence the outcomes of political
struggles or, if economic institutions are imposed on a
population, determine the responses of the population
to these institutions and, hence, ensure their success or
failure. In still other cases, the impact of the cultural
characteristics is to limit the options that are taken into

account by public-policy makers or private individuals. From these brief considerations, it should be clear that a detailed exploration of the mechanisms by which the cultural system influences the economic system is a task that only a researcher willing to do a great deal of work should tackle.

E. Brief Summary

This chapter has shown that nations with the same economic system tend to have the same cultural system as well. I also argue, more tentatively, that among the industrialized OECD nations, the cultural system has had a stronger impact on the economic system than the reverse causation. I placed particular emphasis on the results of a natural experiment created by the division of Germany after World War II. If the economic system determines culture, then the individual cultural characteristics of East and West Germany should have been quite different in 1990. But as shown, once the level of per capita GDP is taken into account, the cultural differences between the two countries were relatively small. I also present more ambiguous evidence that cultural differences can help us understand differences in the transition from a planned to a market economy in Central and Eastern Europe.

Cultural Influences on the Economic System

My argument for the relative strength of cultural determinism does not mean that the economic system is without influence on the cultural system. In particular, the parts of the cultural system concerned with political/social values are those that are the most influenced by the economy and the way in which the economic performance is influenced by the economic system. For instance, a recent study shows that both across countries and over time in the United States, increased wage equality leads a majority of voters to support a more generous welfare state.[17] This topic of economic and social performance is taken up in more detail in Chapter 6.

[17] Erling Barth and Karl O. Moene, "The Equality Multiplier," National Bureau of Economic Research *Working Paper* 15076 (Cambridge MA, NBER, 2009).

— ✤ CHAPTER SIX ✤ —

Do Some Economic Systems Perform Better Than Others?

Generalizations about the economic and social outcomes of economic systems are common, but most are based, as I argue below, on a mistaken view about causation. The problem is sometimes compounded by bias: by selecting a favorable criterion of assessment, it is easy to tailor one's conclusions about the superiority of one system, even though other criteria of assessment might lead to the opposite results. In this chapter, I present a new way of viewing economic systems and their outcomes and employ these ideas to analyze the performance of the four different types of industrial capitalism defined in Chapter 4.

First, we will clear the decks by debunking the conventional wisdom that capitalism is a necessary condition for political freedom. Then the serious work begins with a brief exploration of the problem of causation, which is the key to assessing the economic and social performance of a nation. The subsequent empirical analysis can then be easily carried out, and it yields some unexpected results. The chapter ends with a brief survey of the economic crisis in many industrial capitalist nations that started in 2007/2008.

A. Capitalism and Freedom?

One alleged outcome of capitalism is, as many have claimed, political freedom. Since the early 1960s, however, the relationship between capitalism and freedom has been, for the most part, a relatively closed topic for economists. At that time, Milton Friedman analyzed the "intimate connection between economics and politics" and argued that "only certain combinations of political and economic arrangements are possible" and that political freedom was not possible without capitalism.

Economic freedom is also an indispensable means toward the achievement of political freedom ... Historical evidence speaks with a single voice on the relation between political freedom and a free market. I know of no example in time or place of a society that has been marked by a large measure of political freedom, and that has not also used something comparable to a free market to organize the bulk of its economic activities ... [But] history suggests only that capitalism is a necessary condition for political freedom. Clearly it is not a sufficient condition.[1]

A useful starting point for investigating this hypothesis (which most economists now take for granted) is to see whether nations actually become politically freer as their degree of capitalism increases. For a cross-section of ninety nations in the year 2000, these two variables were closely correlated.[2] This relationship, however, does not imply causality, and if we look at these two variables over time, a much different picture emerges.[3]

Since Friedman suggests that political freedom is not possible without capitalism, I start by focusing on the thirty-three countries in the nineteenth century for

[1] Milton Friedman, *Capitalism and Freedom* (Chicago and London: University of Chicago Press, 1962), 9–10.

[2] Frederic L. Pryor, "Capitalism and Freedom?" *Economic Systems*, 34, no 1: 91–104. The measures for political and capitalism come from the calculations discussed in Chapter 2 and Appendix 2–2.

[3] The degree of "early capitalism" is based, as previously noted, on the calculations of marketization by Irma Adelman and Cynthia Taft Morris (see Appendix 3–1); the political freedom variable is based on the Polity2 variable calculated by Monty G. Marshall and Keith Jaggers (*Polity IV Project: Political Regime Characteristics and Transitions, 1800–2004*: www.cidem.umd.edu/polity, [2005]). Since it is highly correlated with political freedom in 2000, I use it as a proxy for political freedom in the nineteenth century.

which the requisite data are available and which can not be considered capitalist, primarily because their per capita GDP was below the capitalist threshold. Political-freedom scores (estimated by Monty Marshall and Keith Jaggers) range from +10 (high freedom) to −10 (autocracy). If any of these noncapitalist nations have positive political-freedom scores, Friedman's case is disproved. Although some of these noncapitalist countries did have positive political-freedom scores in some years, these periods of freedom did not last long. I have, therefore, only chosen those countries that had positive political-freedom scores for at least fifteen consecutive years and which nevertheless did not appear to pass the capitalist threshold.

Of the thirty-three noncapitalist nations in the sample, nine meet the criterion of a positive political-freedom score; these are listed in Table 6–1. The five nations without exact data on marketization or per capita GDP undoubtedly fell below the capitalist threshold. Among the noncapitalist nations in the sample, Costa Rica provides a telling case. It had political-freedom ratings of +1 from 1841 through 1852, of +3 from 1853 through 1866, of +5 from 1857 through 1889, and of +10 from 1890 through the end of the century, although it did not have a capitalist economic system. Another interesting case is Ethiopia, which had a political-freedom

Table 6–1. *Future Development of Countries with Positive Political Freedom and Low Capitalism Scores in the Nineteenth Century*

Countries with 15 or more consecutive years with Marshall-Jager freedom scores of

	Marketization score, 1900	Per capita GDP, 1900	Capitalism score, 2000	Per Capita GDP, 2000
1 or over				
Bolivia	n.a.	n.a.	−0.53	$2,575
Guatemala	n.a.	n.a.	−0.30	3,396
Korea, South (current area)	3.4	$731	−0.15	14,343
Peru	3.5	817	+0.07	3,686
Serbia	3.7	902	−0.86	2,354
3 or over				
Ethiopia	n.a.	n.a.	n.c.	624
Liberia	n.a.	n.a.	n.c.	847
Orange Free State	4.7	1,440	0.00	4,139
5 or over				
Costa Rica	n.a.	n.a.	+0.05	6,174

Notes: n.a. = data not available; n.c. = not capitalist in 2000.
The political freedom (democracy) scores come from Monty G. Marshall and Keith Jaggers, *Polity IV Project: Political Regime Characteristics and Transitions, 1800–2004* www.cidem.umd.edu/polity. (2005), where countries are rated from −10 (autocracy) to +10 (democracy). The measures of capitalism in 1900 and 2000 are not comparable. The marketization scores are estimated from data from Irma Adelman and Cynthia Taft Morris, "Patterns of Market Expansion in the Nineteenth Century: A Quantitative Study." In George Dalton, ed., *Research in Economic Anthropology* vol. 1 (Greenwich, CT: JAI Press, 1987), 231–325, and run from 0 to 10, with 5.0 considered as borderline capitalist in my analysis. The capitalism scores for 2000 come from Appendix 1–2 and are standardized for the entire 90-country sample classified as capitalist; the scores of all countries have a mean of 0.00 and a standard deviation of one. The per capita GDP data come from Angus Maddison, *The World Economy: Historical Statistics* (Paris: OECD, 2003) and are calculated in 1990 international Geary-Khamis dollars.
The per capita GDP of the area now known as South Korea in 1900 is interpolated. For the Orange Free State, data on per capita income and marketization are for the entire Union of South Africa, and the data for 2000 are for the entire Union of South Africa. For Serbia, the 1900 per capita GDP data are for Yugoslavia as a whole in the same year. Ethiopia includes Eritrea.

rating of +4 from 1866 through 1899 but was not capitalist. And yet neither nation had the alleged necessary economic condition for such political freedom, nor did the other seven nations in the table.

In brief, political freedom can occur without capitalism. I might add that political freedom does not necessarily lead to capitalism since, by 2000, two of these nations still fell below the capitalist threshold. Table 6–1 also suggests that political freedom by itself does not necessarily lead to economic development. Finally, even if political freedom is attained, it is not guaranteed to last. Two of the countries with positive political-freedom scores in the nineteenth century lapsed thereafter, namely Guatemala by the mid-1890s and Liberia by the mid-1880s. Of the nations in Table 6–1 at the end of the twentieth century, the political-freedom scores for some nations, such as Ethiopia and Liberia, were relatively low (0 or 1 on the Marshall-Jager scale) while those of others, such as Peru, fluctuated over the century.

Friedman also appears incorrect when we compare changes in the degree of capitalism and the degree of political freedom for various periods in the nineteenth century.[4] More specifically, there is no statistically

[4] I present the econometric evidence for these claims in "Capitalism and Freedom?" *op. cit.* The data in Appendix 3–4 also show that

significant relationship between *changes* in the degree of capitalism and *changes* in the degree of political freedom. Thus, capitalism and political freedom do not appear to be causally related in this way either. In exploring this relationship I found, however, that both variables are positively related to other variables, such as per capita GDP, and the average level of education. The strong relationship between political freedom and capitalism at any particular point in time appears to arise from their common correlation with these other variables.

B. Two Types of Causation

To see how the varieties of capitalism may influence economic and cultural variables, we need to distinguish two types of causation.

Lineal causation. This directly links economic institutions or policies with performance results. It is familiar to all of us and is illustrated in Part A of Figure 6–1. Here the relation between characteristics G, H, and J with the outcome indicators R and S can be expressed with two

although the degree of capitalism is increasing in the various time intervals for almost all countries, the degree of political freedom significantly increases in only a minority of countries during the same time interval.

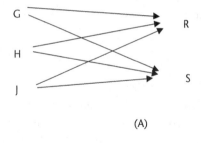

(A)

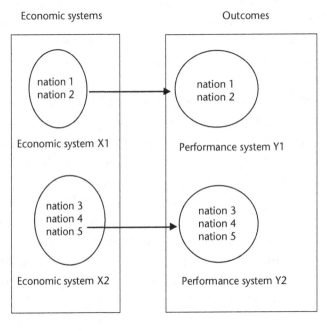

(B)

Figure 6–1. *Two Types of Causation.*

Part A. Lineal causation between variables

Note: G, H, and J are institutional characteristics; R and S are particular outcomes.

Part B. Systemic causation

Note: X1 and X2 represent particular economic systems (composed of particular institutional characteristics); and Y1 and Y2, their performance systems (composed of particular outcomes).

equations: $aG + bH + cJ = R$ and $dG + eH + fJ = S$, where the lowercase letters indicate the relative importance that characteristics G, H, and J independently have in determining the outcomes R and S. If the situation becomes more complicated, that is, where there is reciprocal causation between G, H, and J or between R and S, then more equations, more variables, and some sophisticated statistical techniques are needed in order to identify the causal role of each variable.

Systemic causation. This is presented in Part B of Figure 6–1. It shows two different types of economic systems, X1 and X2, which are related respectively to two types of performance systems, Y1 and Y2, with the economic systems defined in terms of clusters of particular institutional characteristics and the performance systems defined in terms of clusters of outcomes (such as economic growth, unemployment, inflation, and the distribution of income).

The various countries embodying these economic and performance systems are labeled by number. Since the same countries are in the corresponding economic and performance systems, we can say that economic systems X1 and X2 respectively cause performance systems Y1 and Y2, other things being equal. Just as it is not individual muscles, blood vessels, and organs that determine how a human body functions, the various characteristics in a given country do not independently play a causal role; rather, it is their interaction with other characteristics as a component of the economic system that leads to particular outcomes.

Systemic causation can also be supplemented by taking into account additional causal variables. For instance, suppose that high-income nations with a particular economic system are associated with a set of variables indicating economic performance, but the low income nations with the same economic system are not. If we consider all the nations with that economic system, we see that the system is not associated with these particular performance indicators. To get meaningful results, systemic causation must be analyzed by holding the per capita GDP of the various nations constant.

This description of systemic causation does not, of course, take into account reciprocal influences between the economic and performance systems, but to do so would require a much more complex analysis and data that would be very difficult to obtain for our OECD sample nations. Thus, we must see how far we can go with the more parsimonious approach illustrated in Part B of Figure 6–1.

In the past, a common way of avoiding the issue of systemic causation was to select the key variables and then model causation in a lineal fashion. For instance, instead of dealing with performance of capitalist and communist economic systems in their entirety, an analyst might define the key economic-systems variables as the degree of public ownership and the performance indicator as the economic growth rate. Such a method has advantages for evaluating economic systems: it eliminates a great deal of statistical clutter by allowing the system to be defined in a simple quantitative fashion and by considering the economic growth rate as "typical" for all types of economic performance. But several grave disadvantages are also apparent: Regarding the economic system, we have no assurance that the arbitrarily selected key variable is an adequate characterization of the entire system; moreover, its impact is not distinguished from that of any other characteristic defining the system. Regarding the performance system, we also have no assurance that the arbitrarily selected performance variable is really a "typical outcome."

The case for focusing on systemic rather than lineal causation was summarized by Aristotle more than 2,300 years ago, in *Metaphysics*: "A whole … is something over and above the parts."[5] The effects produced

---

[5] Aristotle, *Metaphysics*, Book 8, 1045a, line 10. Some important implications of this idea in the social sciences are analyzed by Peter Corning in *Holistic Darwinism: Synergy, Cybernetics, and the Bioeconomics of Evolution* (Chicago: University of Chicago Press, 2005), 51, 65.

by whole economic systems are greater (and different) than that produced by their individual institutional characteristics.

C. Performance Systems

To estimate performance systems using a cluster analysis, I assembled thirty-eight economic and social-output indicators from a variety of readily available sources. Twenty-two of these indicators concern strictly economic performance (for instance, growth of per capita GDP, inflation, unemployment rates, rate of labor strikes, and debt), while sixteen refer to social/economic performance (for instance, income inequality, murder rates, educational achievement, life expectancy, and health). I tried, whenever possible, to select indicators for which data are available for all or almost all of the sample OECD nations in about 1990;[6] these indicators are listed in Table 6–3.

Let us now define a performance system in the same manner as the economic and cultural systems, using

---

[6] Most of the indicators for Germany are exclusively for West Germany. For several social indicators indicated in Table 6–2, however, separating the two German nations proved impossible and the data refer to both East and West Germany.

Table 6-2. Cultural, Economic, and Performance Systems of the OECD Nations around 1990

	Cultural Systems	Economic Systems	Performance Systems
No. of indicators	41	40	38
Unexplained Variation	44.7%	52.2%	52.4%
	Mostly Anglo-Saxon (MAS-C)	*Mostly Anglo-Saxon (MAS-E)*	*Mostly Anglo-Saxon (MAS-P)*
	Canada	Canada	Canada
	Ireland	Ireland	Ireland
	UK	UK	UK
	USA	USA?	USA.
	no data	Australia	Australia
	no data	New Zealand	New Zealand?
	Switzerland?	–	–
	Nordic (NO-C)	*Nordic (NO-E)*	*North\West Europe (NWE-P)*
	Denmark	Denmark	Denmark
	Norway	Norway	Norway
		Sweden	Sweden
	Sweden	Finland	Finland
	–	–	
	–	–	
	–	–	

West Europe (WE-C)	West Europe (WE-E)	Austria
Austria	Austria	Netherlands
Netherlands	Netherlands	West Germany
West Germany	West Germany	Belgium
–	Belgium	
Finland	Switzerland?	
	–	

South Europe (SE-C)	South Europe (SE-E)	South Europe (SE-Pa)
Italy	Italy	Italy
Portugal	Portugal	Portugal
Spain	Spain	Spain
France	France	France?
no data	Greece	–
Belgium	–	–

		South Europe (SE-Pb)
		Greece

Other (O-C)	Other (O-E)	Other (O-P)
Japan	Japan	Japan
–	–	Switzerland

Note: All calculations are made for five clusters. Data for the cultural and economic systems come from Table 4–1 and the labels of the systems are the geographical location of the majority of nations; the letters after the geographical areas distinguish slightly different groups of countries. The unexplained variation in the cluster analysis measured the variance from the cluster centers. The performance indicators for Germany are mostly for the former West Germany.

the various performance indicators as the elements of the system. More specifically, we apply a cluster analysis to the various performance indicators to determine that the optimal number of clusters is five. I have therefore grouped the nations into five economic systems, as in Chapter 5, so that it would be easier to determine if the same nations were in the corresponding economic and performance systems. The country compositions of these economic and performance systems are presented in Table 6–2, and, for comparison, the cultural systems from Table 5–1 are also included.

The parallelisms between all three systems should be evident. To determine whether such parallelism is statistically significant, it is necessary to calculate the percentage of countries that are in parallel clusters and then to estimate the statistical significance of this percentage. In making this calculation, however, a difficulty arises because the economic and cultural systems yield separate clusters for the *Nordic* and *West European* nations, while the performance clusters united them into a single cluster. If we combine the economic systems of the *Nordic* and *West European* economic systems, 90.5 percent of the nations in the economic and performance systems are in the same clusters (88.9 percent if countries with questionable systemic designations are removed). Both of these are statistically significant (at the 0.01 level of confidence) and are much larger than what we would expect from a random process. In turn, these results establish a causal linkage between economic system and performance outcomes.

Because different countries with the same economic system often pursue very different policies, we would reasonably expect them to have different outcomes. It is, therefore, surprising that the degree of parallelism between the economic system and the performance system is not considerably lower than between the cultural system and economic system. The unexplained variation measures the difference between the country points and the center of each cluster: This statistic is roughly the same for the performance systems as for the institutional indicators determining the economic systems, and only slightly higher than the indicators for the cultural systems.

The key conclusion is that there is an important parallelism between the economic and performance systems and that a causal link is apparent. In Chapter 5 I argue that the cultural system has a major causal influence on the type of economic system. This leads us to the following tentative chain of causation: cultural systems => economic systems => performance systems. Although more research and statistical analysis is necessary to establish a solid base for this proposed causal chain, it meets our intuitive expectations.

The next step is equally important, namely, testing whether the economic system plays a causal role in determining the *individual characteristics* of the performance system,

D. Further Exploration of the Characteristics of the Performance Systems

Although each economic system is correlated with a specific bundle of performance outcomes, it is also important to examine the relationship between the economic systems and the components of the performance system. For instance, does a particular economic system explain the faster or slower growth rate of a particular nation? Table 6–3 presents the various characteristics of the performance systems and designates whether the values for those characteristics are significantly higher or lower for that system than for other OECD nations when the per capita GDP is held constant.[7] This is a procedure similar to that followed in Tables 4–2 and 3–2.

---

[7] I calculated regressions of the following sort: $C_{Yi} = a + bS_{Xi} + cYCap_i$, where C_{Yi} is a single performance characteristic of system Y of country i, S_{Xi} is a 0–1 (dummy) variable of the economic system of country 1, $YCap_i$ is the per capita GDP of country i, and a, b, and c are calculated coefficients.

Do Some Economic Systems Perform Better?

For the various economic indicators, it is surprising that so few of the countries in the individual performance systems feature significantly higher or lower values. Omitting Greece (South Europe-Pb) and Japan/Switzerland (O-P), which contain respectively one and two countries, only nine cases reveal significantly different average values for the strictly economic performance indicators for the twenty-three indicators. Moreover, several, such as the levels of pollution and greenhouse gases, are really due to policies unrelated to economic system.[8] The key conclusions are that systemic differences did not seem the key factor influencing many economic outcomes and that no system is unambiguously better.

By contrast, for the fourteen social/economic characteristics, seven show significant differences between the first three performance systems. This is because these indicators are more likely to reflect values and other cultural characteristics. The *mostly Anglo-Saxon* nations have more adults working in groups to aid the poor) and more

---

[8] However, highly detailed institutional data from Olof Bäckman ("Institutions, Structures and Poverty – A Comparative Study of 16 countries, 1980–2000," *European Sociological Review* 25, no. 2, 2009: 251–64) show that certain micro-institutions have a significant impact on the poverty rate and, hence, on the distribution of low incomes.

Table 6–3. *OECD Outcome Statistics*

	Mostly Anglo-Saxon-P	North/West Europe-P	South Europe-Pa	Greece (South Europe-Pb)	Japan/ Switzerland (O-P)
Volume of per capita GDP, 1980–2000					
Average annual growth rate	–	–	–	Low	–
Coefficient of variation of annual growth rates	–	–	–	High	–
Correlation coefficient: last year = s and this year = s growth rate	–	–	–	–	–
GDP deflator, 1980–2000					
Average annual increase	–	–	High	–	–
Coefficient of variation of annual increase	–	–	–	–	High
Correlation coefficient: last year = s and this year = s increase	–	–	–	–	–
Unemployment rate, 1980–2000					
Average annual unemployment rate	–	–	–	–	–

Coefficient of variation of annual unemployment rates			—	—	—
Correlation coefficient: last year = s and this year = s rate			—	—	—
Inequality of disposable income, 1990					
Ratio of income: 10th percentile to 50th percentile	Low	High	—	Low	—
Ratio of income: 90th percentile to 50th percentile	High	Low	—	—	—
General economic indicators					
Ratio of net exports of goods and services to GDP, 1980–2000	High	High	—	—	—
Ratio of all government deficits to GDP, 1990–2000			—	—	—
Average annual money market interest rates, 1980–2000			—	High	—
Coefficient of variation of annual money market interest rates, 1980–2000			—	—	High

(continued)

Table 6–3. (*Continued*)

	Mostly Anglo-Saxon-P	North/West Europe-P	South Europe-Pa	Greece (South Europe-Pb)	Japan/Switzerland (O-P)
Ratio of consumer debt to GDP, mid 1990s	–	–	–	–	–
Greater output per unit of additional investment, 1980–2000	High	–	–	–	–
Work and enterprise indicators					
Days lost in strikes per total workers, 1988–1992	–	–	–	High	–
Impact of absenteeism from work (scale from 0 to 100), c. 1990	–	–	–	–	High
Lost work days per 1000 workers. from accidents, manufacturing sector, c. 1990	–	–	–	–	–
Greenhouse gases (CO_2 equiv.) per 1000 pop., GDP constant, 1990	High	–	–	–	–

Average index values of other air pollution (NO$_x$, CO, SO$_x$)	High	—	Low	—	—
Adjusted domestic patents per 1000 adults, 1988–92	—	—	—	—	—

SOCIAL/ECONOMIC PERFORMANCE INDICATORS

Social indicators, general

Percentage of children in single parent families, c.1990	—	—	—	—	Low
Suicides per 100,000 population, 1990	—	High	—	—	—
Murders per 100,000 population in the period 1988–92	—	—	—	—	—
Nonlethal crimes per 100,000 reported in victim statistics, 1988–1999	High	—	—	n.a.	—

Indicators of educational achievement

Intnl. adult literacy scores (prose, document, quant.), mid-1990s	—	High	Low	n.a.	—

(continued)

Table 6-3. (*Continued*)

	Mostly Anglo-Saxon-P	North/West Europe-P	South Europe-Pa	Greece (South Europe-Pb)	Japan/ Switzerland (O-P)
Coeff. of variation of intnl. adult literacy scores, mid-1990s	—	—	—	n.a.	n.a.
Scores of 13-year-olds (math, reading, science)	—	—	—	—	—
Health indicators					
Average life expectancy, 1988–1992	—	—	—	—	High
Infant mortality per 1000 births, 1988–1992	—	—	—	—	—
Percentage of low-weight babies, 1988–1992	—	Low	—	—	—
Maternal deaths per 1000 live births, 1988–1992	—	—	—	n.a.	—
Indicators of social capital					
% of adults eng. in comm. activ. at least once a month, mid-1990s	—	—	—	n.a	—

Avg. no. groups adults belong to with a redist. purp., c. 1990	High	—	—	n.a.
Avg. no. groups adults belong to with a social purp. c. 1990	—	High	—	n.a.

Notes: n.a. = data not available.

The country composition of the clusters is presented in Table 6–1. The calculations, however, exclude France and New Zealand since classification of these two nations is questionable. "High" indicates that the value for the countries in the cluster for that particular indicator is significantly higher than for the other OECD nations, holding per capita GDP constant; "low" indicates the reverse. Sources of the data and actual values are presented in Frederic L. Pryor, "Systems as Causal Forces," *Journal of Economic Behavior and Organization* 67, no. 3 (September 2008): 545–59.

The coefficient of variation is a percentage measure of the spread of the indicators in various countries. The correlation coefficient runs from 0 (no relationship) to 1 (the variables run exactly parallel to each other) and measures how close the variables under consideration are related. The GDP deflator measures the average price increases of all goods and services. The coefficient of variation ranges from 0 (no variation) to infinity. NO_x and SO_x measure various nitrates and sulfates. Disp. = disposable. Quant. Designates quantitative reasoning. "Adults eng. in comm. activ" = "adults engaged in community activities." "redist. purp." = "redistributive purpose."

nonlethal crimes. The *North/West European* nations have higher adult literacy scores, fewer low-weight babies, but more suicides. The *South European* (SE-Pa) nations have lower adult literacy scores.

It is, of course, possible to include other performance variables,[9] but it is difficult to obtain comparable data for all of the countries in the OECD sample. For instance, in a statistical analysis of sixteen European nations, transaction costs (the costs of enforcing contracts, coordinating the production of goods and services, and selling them) are significantly higher in the two *mostly Anglo-Saxon* nations in that sample than in the *Nordic* nations, while nations with *West* and *South European* economic systems fall somewhere in between.[10] This means, for instance, that for each worker actually producing goods and services, the *Nordic* nations have fewer workers in the "overhead" activities. Unfortunately, only two of

---

[9] Table 6–3 includes only very general social indicators. Some studies which include indicators that focus on quite narrow social phenomena, such as child poverty and infant mortality, do show systemic differences. See, for example, the international comparisons presented by Marque-Louisa Miringoff and Sandra Opdycke in *America's Social Health* (Armong, NY: M. E. Sharpe, 2008).

[10] Frederic L. Pryor, "Transaction Costs on a National Level: Causes and Consequences," *Journal of Institutional and Theoretical Economics* 164, no. 4 (December/2008): 676–95

the eight *mostly Anglo-Saxon* nations are included in this European sample, so we must consider such results as tentative.

In brief, this discussion shows for the indicators under examination that the strictly economic outcomes of the four types of capitalism are not greatly different. Thus, we cannot say that one system is clearly superior to another in purely economic terms. But these systems do differ in their social/economic outcomes, although it is difficult to attribute this to the system per se. Judgments about the superiority of a given system, however, depend upon our value judgments, since most of the systems manifest both more and less desirable social outcomes.

E. The Recent Economic Crisis of Industrial Capitalist Nations

As I write, it is too early to be able to determine the different ways in which nations with the four economic systems have performed during the economic crisis that began in 2007/2008. Moreover, some nations have suffered, not because of any defect in their economic system, but because they are dependent on trade and their exports have fallen. For this reason I focus on the industrial capitalist nations as a whole.

1. Some General Considerations

A capitalist economic system does not ensure rapid or smooth economic growth. According to Adam Smith, market economies are primarily guided by an "invisible hand," but this does not necessarily mean optimal macroeconomic performance, especially since subjective factors (sometimes called "animal spirits") play a crucial role. For instance, if economic confidence is low, then business investment may be low and, hence, economic growth will be low. If public sentiment swings between optimism and pessimism, the economy may experience fluctuations. Those who proclaimed the "great moderation" of business fluctuations in the 1980s and 1990s turned out to be mythmaking. Increasingly, economists are emphasizing the importance of subjective factors influencing macroeconomic, and the subdiscipline of behavioral economics has begun to make important contributions to economic analysis on these issues by focusing sharp attention on them.

Looking at production of goods and services, John Maynard Keynes pointed out in 1936 that no automatic mechanism ensures that planned savings (based on the subjective decisions of income receivers) and planned investment (also based on the subjective evaluations) will be equal so that full employment will result.[11] The idea

[11] John Maynard Keynes, *The General Theory of Employment, Interest, and Money* (New York: Harcourt, Brace, 1936).

that consumers save in a rational manner has also lost credibility; and economists are increasingly emphasizing that investment also depends on views of the future, which can change radically in a short period.[12]

Economic forecasting is difficult when planned savings and investment are not equal, especially when the psychological factors underlying these plans can not be easily fathomed. Given these problems, it is not difficult to understand why few economists were able to foresee the seriousness of the coming world recession.

A more recent line of investigation focuses primary attention, not directly on the behavior of saving and investment or the production of goods and services, but on economic behavior in the financial sector. For instance, some have argued that after several years of good economic times, investors begin to believe that such conditions will last for a long time and, for this reason, take increasing risks in order to capture ever higher economic gains.[13] As the amount of debt held by these investors increases in proportion to the assets they will

[12] A recent and useful summary of this literature is George A. Akerlof and Robert J. Shiller, *Animal Spirits: How Human Psychology Drives the Economy and Why it Matters for Global Capitalism* (Princeton, NJ: Princeton University Press, 2009).

[13] This discussion follows the ideas of Hyman Minsky in *Stabilizing an Unstable Economy* (New York: McGraw Hill, 2008) and his follower Robert J. Barbera, *The Cost of Capitalism* (New York: McGraw Hill, 2009).

use to pay them off in the future (financial leverage rises), the financial system becomes ever more fragile so that a small incident, such as the bankruptcy of a few large companies, can start a chain reaction: creditors perceiving a rise in risk try to call in their loans, which results in frantic sales of assets, a fall in asset prices, and more bankruptcies. This plunging spiral, in turn, leads to a fall in investment and income (the mechanism described by Keynes), which adds to the downward pressures on production. Again, although the increasing financial leverage in most industrialized, capitalist nations after 1995 was well-known, few saw the critical point of the process in 2007/2008 and the extent to which production would fall and unemployment would rise thereafter.

In addition to these subjective factors, certain aspects of managerial pay and incentives in financial institutions can induce their executives to make long-term risky investments. This is especially likely if executives are compensated in terms of the short-term gains they bring to the company or if they are protected by generous severance packages that are not tied to the long-term results of their decisions.[14]

---

[14] Richard Posner, *A Failure of Capitalism: The Crisis of '08 and the Descent into Depression* (Cambridge, MA: Harvard University Press, 009). Chapter 3 has a useful discussion of these "rational" reasons for excessive risk taking by financial institutions.

Because of the role of subjective factors, capitalist economic systems are, in brief, fragile and experience aggregate production fluctuations. The key questions are why these fluctuations are usually small but, in rare cases, are great enough to severely impact production and consumption in one or many nations.

2. Recent Events

The current capitalist world economic crisis began in the United States, where in the early years of the twenty-first century, interest rates were low and saving had declined. The scramble of financial institutions to increase profits led to loose credit and the ever-increasing leveraging of their capital. Easy borrowing led to a bubble in the housing market and, to a lesser extent, the stock and other asset markets as well. When the housing bubble burst in 2006–7, that is, when the buildup in the inventory of unsold houses became apparent to a wide public, housing prices fell sharply, and some homeowners – unable to sell their homes to pay off their mortgages – went bankrupt or walked away from their homes. This, in turn, placed great strain on mortgage lenders, and after Lehman Brothers bank went bankrupt in 2008, credit flows froze as other financial institutions declined to take the risk of lending more. The downward spiral was exacerbated by the high ratio of debt to assets (financial leverage) that could not be easily sold without loss. Such risky assets were held by many financial institutions, whose officials believed that the probabilities of a depression were so remote that they could afford the higher risks brought about by higher leveraging of their assets. As in the Great Depression of the 1930s, financial institutions played a key role in the economic downturn and subsequent decline in production. Parallels include the easy credit that was available in the 1920s, the ensuing stock market bubble and its bursting in late 1929, and the bankruptcy of important banks, such as the Kreditanstalt of Vienna in 1931.

The recent financial crisis in the United States was rapidly paralleled in other industrial nations, in part because they were involved in the U.S. mortgage market (and the holding of dubious mortgage-backed securities). In many cases their financial institutions were even more highly leveraged than the U.S.-based institutions; in addition, exports in many countries fell because of lack of trade credits or because the United States was one of their largest trade partners. By the fourth quarter of 2009, almost most OECD nation experienced a falling GDP over the last two years, with only Australia and Norway experiencing any significant GDP growth.[15]

The impact of the economic system on the response of nations to these events varied enormously among nations

[15] Quarterly data on GDP come from the OECD Web site: www.oecd.org.

with the same economic system. Among the countries with a *mostly Anglo-Saxon* economic system, some performance variables were quite different, for instance, Canada had no bank failures (although its GDP fell at about the same rate as that of the USA),; and, as noted above, Australia's GDP actually increased. Among the nations with a *Nordic* economic system, Norway performed much better than Sweden, which suggestion, which suggests that the role of governmental and business policies may play a more important role than the system per se.

Business cycles and financial crises are not an artifact of the past, and we see now that a nation's financial institutions and policies are critical determinants of its economic performance. But the agonized and belated confession in 2008 of Alan Greenspan, a former chairman of the U.S. Federal Reserve, that the financial system cannot successfully regulate itself to avoid such crises does not, unfortunately, tell us what institutions to build, what regulations should be implemented, and what policies should be taken to avoid future economic crises.

F. Interpreting Problems of Systemic Causation

The concept of systemic causation raises some serious issues: How exactly does such causation manifest itself?

What is the mechanism of causation? What is the exact interaction of the various characteristics of the system? Are there additional causal mechanisms at work, other than those I have described, that might bring about changes in the systems? How important is reverse causation? On a less abstract level, what exactly does it mean that the economic systems have a significant impact on performance systems as a whole, but not on most of the individual indicators that define the entire system? Similarly, what does it mean that the cultural systems have a significant impact on economic systems, even though only a few of the individual values composing the cultural system have a significant relationship with any given economic system? At this point there may be no definite answers, but there are some promising paths to explore.

Within any given system there are trade-offs between outcomes. For instance, in a given performance system an interest rate that does not vary very much over time might have an impact on economic growth, or unemployment, or the trade deficit. These trade-offs are, however, structured and constrained by the economic system, so that certain outcomes seem more likely than others. For instance, an economic system with considerable variation of employment over time is unlikely to have low social supports for the unemployed. Since policy or institutional trade-offs can take place in several dimensions, a particular economic system might not have a significant impact on any particular outcome, even though it exercises an influence on the set of outcomes, which are related to each other. Determining the exact causal impact of a single institution of an economic system also raises problems because its causal impact depends upon the presence of other characteristics within the system. Even the origin of a particular institution in the economic system is sometimes problematic. For instance, in the cultural domain, a certain value in one cultural system might play a role in the formation of particular institutions of an economic system, while its presence in another cultural system might play a role in the formation of a quite different economic institution.[16] A biological analogy to this argument may provide insight. Both humans and horses possess a set of genes [containing the DNA sequence (homeobox)] that create legs, but the interaction of these genes with other genes determines whether horse or human legs will emerge at birth. So the presence of particular genes may not be correlated

---

[16] This can be seen more concretely in Part B of Figure 6–1. The presence of a characteristic G in system 1 in the economic system X1 may play a role in the creation of performance system Y1 and its presence in economic system X2 may play a role in the creation of performance system Y2.

with specific species, even though an entire set of genes definitely is.

Finally, it must be emphasized that lineal and systemic causation models can be complementary. It is possible that greater explanatory power can be gained if exogenous variables are introduced into the systemic analysis, for instance, the level of economic development, the size of the country, or the heterogeneity of its population. Moreover, the two types of causal analysis can focus on different but related problems. For example, the composition of inventories held by a specific manufacturing company may be determined in large part by its specific industry. Although a systemic-causation approach using various characteristics of a group of industries to derive clusters of different industries may indicate inventories in the automobile industry are higher or lower than that in clothing industry, a lineal-causal analysis of firms within the automobile industry may tell you whether the inventories of a particular company making cars are higher or lower than those of companies making trucks.

G. Brief Reflections

In this chapter, I argue that various performance indicators are complementary to each other, making it possible to delineate performance systems, like cultural and economic systems, through a cluster analysis. Comparison of all three systems reveals a statistically significant parallelism in the country composition.

The most important empirical result described in this chapter is that economic system had a considerable impact on social/economic outcomes but had much of one on the purely economic performance outcomes. Tests of lineal causation were less successful: the economic systems have little predictive power for the individual performance characteristics, and conversely, the individual characteristics of the economic systems do not very well predict the performance systems. The causal chain at work appears to be: cultural systems ⇒ economic systems ⇒ performance systems (clusters of performance outcomes), although the last link in the chain is more apparent in the social/economic indicators than in the narrower economic indicators.

This demonstration that in certain cases a system can play a causal role, independent of any particular variable (characteristic), means that we need to be more careful in examining economic causation. For instance, recent research suggests that legal systems are linked to political and economic systems.[17] Other possible applications are for enterprise financial systems or management

[17] Edward L. Glaeser and Andrei Shleifer, "Legal Origins," *Quarterly Journal of Economics* 117, no. 2 (2002): 1193–1229.

systems, which are composed of many characteristics. Instead of the standard econometric analyses of firm performance, we need to consider whether these systems might be playing a causal role alongside the other variables that are under consideration in determining a firm's outcomes. Many other possibilities for research and analysis also suggest themselves: Why do the same fiscal or monetary policies have different effects in particular countries? If we include variables indicating the economic systems of these countries, we may find that such policies operate differently in one economic system than they do in another.

Despite the obvious advantages of exploring systemic causation, few theoretical models include the concept. Therefore, any use of systemic variables has usually been an inductive and ad hoc procedure – just as mine has been. I provide no theoretical discussion of why the cultural values, the economic institutions, or the performance indicators form systems, or why these systems have causal impacts. For that matter, we have few theories at present about why certain goods or variables or institutions are complementary and, instead, must rely upon statistical evidence to tell us that they are. So here we have used a similar empirical approach in unearthing systemic causation in cultural, economic, and performance domains.

Do Some Economic Systems Perform Better?

Up to now economists have focused almost exclusively on lineal causation. Now we need to consider other ways in which the complex subject of our inquiry, capitalism, functions. I hope to have shown in this chapter how such inductive research might be carried out. To paraphrase the Aristotle quotation cited above, social wholes (cultural, economic, or performance systems) are greater than the sum of their parts; and understanding their performance must take into account the configuration of all their components, not just a few.

CHAPTER SEVEN

Happiness and Economic Systems

The objectively measured performance of different types of capitalism tells only part of the story. Let's turn now to a more subjective measure: happiness. How happy are the people living in these economic systems? And is one type of capitalism more likely to create happiness than another?

Various studies on the determinants of happiness (or subjective well-being, as it is sometimes called) in different nations have focused on the impact of particular demographic variables and also of certain economic performance outcomes, such as unemployment and inflation. Others have also investigated the impact on happiness of political performance measures, such as the efficiency of government services, the degree of civil liberties, or recently, the presence of a particular political system.[1] If political systems have an impact on happiness, why should we not suppose that economic systems have a similar impact and, therefore, look for the key economic institutions that bring about such results?

Scholars have made little attempt to find such links between happiness and economic systems, and I suspect that most of them are dubious about such a relationship. By contrast, the issue of happiness and the type of capitalism is often raised in the popular media, and we find two main lines of speculation:

1. *Ideological.* Many left-wing commentators assert that happiness is greatest in "gentle welfare states," such as those with a *Nordic* economic system, and is lowest in countries with a *mostly Anglo-Saxon* economic

---

[1] Bruno S. Frey and Alois Stutzer have shown that subjective well-being varies between Swiss cantons according to the degree of direct democracy. See Frey, *Happiness: A Revolution in Economics* (Cambridge, MA: MIT Press, 2008); Frey and Stutzer, *Happiness and Economics: How the Economy and Institutions Affect Well-Being* (Princeton, NJ: Princeton University Press, 2002); and Frey and Stutzer, "Happiness, Economy and Institutions," *Economic Journal* 110 (October 2000): 918–38. John Helliwell and Haifang Huang provide cross-country evidence that citizens are happier in nations with constitutions establishing a strong president, some form of

system with their alleged "dog-eat-dog" style of capitalism. Right-wing commentators assert the opposite,
that the economic system of the *Nordic* nations stifles
initiative and frustrates those who wish to improve
their lives, while lasses-faire capitalism allows them
to reach their greatest potential and thus become
happier. The empirical analysis below provides little
support for either view.

2. *Pragmatic.* Some claim that the path to national happiness is not as simple as the ideologues claim and
that abstract economic ideologies are irrelevant to
most people. Instead, they argue that the population
views the economic system instrumentally, that is,
that people really care about the performance of the
system, and not the system per se. Since Chapter 5
shows that the four capitalist economic systems perform almost equally well on most economic criteria,
we would expect to find little difference between the

proportional voting, and efficient governments. These stud-
ies include Helliwell, "How's Life? Combining Individual and
National Variables to Explain Subjective Well-Being," National
Bureau of Economic Research *Working Paper* no. 9065 (Cambridge,
MA: NBER, 2002); and Helliwell and Huang, "How's Your
Government? International Evidence Linking Good Government
and Well-Being," National Bureau of Economic Research *Working
Paper* no. 11988 (Cambridge, MA: NBER, 2006).

happiness of people in countries with one system and those with another. This turns out to be the case, as we shall see.

In order to separate the effect of the political environment from that of the economic system, I explore a sample of industrialized OECD nations in the 1990s. These countries have different economic institutions and systems but relatively similar degrees of political freedom and resemble each other in many other aspects of their political systems. By confining ourselves to nations that are roughly similar on the political side but have quite different economic systems, we can easily explore various cultural and economic factors with more confidence that the results are not driven by unspecified causal variables on the political side.

A key problem is, of course, the measurement of average happiness in a nation, and I discuss this in the next section. Then I survey fifty-three possible determinants of happiness on a national level and explain how they can be reduced to a manageable number by searching for their common elements (through a "principal component" analysis). Then I present the results of my attempt to relate the economic system to the level of happiness, holding other determinants of happiness constant. This is followed by a refutation of several objections to this type of analysis. Finally, I summarize the results and explore in greater detail why economic systems do not influence happiness, whereas political systems do.

A. Measuring Happiness in a Nation

Hundreds of public opinion surveys from countries throughout the world pose questions of the following type: All things considered, how happy would you say that you are on a scale from 0 through 10? Sometimes the question is asked in terms of "life satisfaction" rather than happiness, but the results are roughly the same. The results of most of these surveys have been standardized and summarized in the World Database of Happiness.[2]

Several serious questions can be immediately raised about the meaningfulness of the survey responses: Are people telling the truth? Do the various happiness or subjective well-being scores yield comparable results

---

[2] Ruut Veenhoven et al., "Freedom and Happiness: A Comparative Study in Forty-Four Nations in the Early 1990s." In Ed Diener and Eunkook M. Suh, eds., *Culture and Subjective Well-being* (Cambridge, MA: MIT Press, 2000), 257–88; and Ruut Veenhoven et al., "World Database of Happiness," www.worlddatabaseofhappiness.eur.nl. (1994). The latter source presents various surveys throughout the world and shows that the wording of the question makes little difference.

across individuals and societies? Are people's answers consistent over time? Are international comparisons of these answers biased by cultural norms concerning the propriety of talking about one's individual happiness? The social science literature on happiness has explored such questions at considerable length, and the general consensus is that in industrial nations, the answers to these survey questions do reflect an important reality that is independent of cultural differences and that can be meaningfully compared from country to country.[3] Let's proceed on this assumption.

[3] For instance, by P. Ouweenel and Ruut Veenhoven in "Cross-national Differences in Happiness: Cultural Bias or Societal Quality?" pp. 168–84 in Nico Bleichrodt and Pieter J. D. Drenth, eds., *Contemporary Issues in Cross-Cultural Psychology* (Amsterdam: Swets and Zeitlinger, 1991); Ed Diener and Carol Diener, "Most People Are Happy," *Psychological Science* 7 (1996): 181–85; Diener and Suh, *op. cit.*; Ed Diener and Richard E. Lucas, "Personality and Subjective Well-Being,": 213–29 in Daniel Kahneman, Ed Diener, and Norbert Schwarz, eds., *Well-Being: The Foundations of Hedonic Psychology* (New York: Russell Sage Foundation, 1999); Veenhoven et al., *op. cit.*; Ruut Veenhoven, "Quality-of-Life in Individualistic Society: A Comparison in 43 Nations in the Early 1990's," *Social Indicators Research* 48, no. 2 (1999): 157–86; Frey and Stutzer *op. cit.*; Ruut Veenhoven, "Comparability of Happiness across Nations" (2008) www.eur.nl/fsw/research/veenhoven/Pub2000s/2008f–full-pdf; and many others. For cultural differences and happiness, see Robert Diener, Robert Biswas, Joar Vittersø, and Ed Diener

The happiness data that I have used below are from a summary essay by Ruut Veenhoven and Wim Kalmijn and represent arithmetical averages of the results, reported in the World Database of Happiness, from many different surveys taken during the 1990s. These data for the OECD nations are presented in Table 7–1 along with per capita GDP and economic system.[4]

B. Possible Determinants of Happiness on a National Level

Table 7–1 shows that the average level of happiness does not greatly vary from one economic system to another. The nations with *Nordic* and *South European* economic systems averages appear to be significantly different, but if we hold the logarithm of the per capita GDP constant and rerun the regressions, none of the systems proves to have a significantly different average level of happiness. Although the happiness ratings of the countries in the sample appear to

in "Most People Are Pretty Happy, but There Is Cultural Variation: The Inughuit, the Amish, and the Maasai," *Journal of Happiness Studies* 6, no. 3 (2005): 205–26.

[4] The importance of per capita GDP is discussed by Betsey Stevenson and Justin Wolfers, "Economic Growth and Subjective Well-Being: Reassessing the Easterlin Paradox" http://bpp.wharton.upenn.edu/betseys/papers/happiness.pdf (2008).

Table 7–1. Basic Data on Happiness for the 1990s

Country	Average Happiness Level	Per Capita GDP 1993–97	Country	Average Happiness Level	Per Capita GDP 1993–97
A. Nations with a Mostly Anglo-Saxon Economic System			*B. Nations with a Nordic Economic System*		
Australia	7.3	$23,970	Denmark	8.0	$25,539
Canada	7.6	23,376	Finland	7.5	21,279
Ireland	7.8	19,596	Norway	7.4	29,669
Japan	6.2	24,819	Sweden	7.6	22,558
New Zealand	7.4	18,705	Average	7.63	24,761
Switzerland?	8.0	29,152			
U.K.	7.2	23,107			
U.S.	7.4	30,132			
Average	7.36	24,107			
C. Nations with a West European Economic System			*D. Nations with a South European Economic System*		
Austria	7.0	24,875	Greece	6.3	14,857
Belgium	7.3	24,428	Italy	6.9	23,411
France?	6.6	24,070	Portugal	6.7	15,750
Germany	7.1	23,390	Spain	6.6	18,434
Netherlands	7.6	25,804	Average	6.63	18,113
Average	7.12	24,513			

Notes: The happiness data are calculated on a scale from 0 through 10 and come from Ruut Veenhoven and Wim Kalmijn, "Inequality-Adjusted Happiness in Nations: Egalitarianism and Utilitarianism Married Together in a New Index of Societal Performance," *Journal of Happiness Studies* 6, no. 4/2005: 421–55. Per capita GDP is in constant international dollars and come from the World Bank, *World Development Indicators* www.worldbank.org (2008). The classification of the systems and the meaning of the question marks are explained in Chapter 4.

be roughly similar, for many countries outside the sample, the happiness ratings are far different.

Although the attempt to link the level of happiness to the economic system does not seem very promising, we have not, of course, examined the impact of other causal variables except per capita GDP. Two major problems arise, however, when we try to carry out such a statistical exploration. First, some determinants of happiness are correlated, so their separate impacts cannot be easily assessed. Second, there are too many possible determinants of happiness to examine at the same time for just these twenty-one nations.

The first difficulty is illustrated in a useful and interesting study showing that the happiness of nations is significantly related to a number of measures of freedom, that is, to the opportunity and capacity to make economic, political, and personal choices.[5] But when per capita GDP is held constant, it turns out that only the correlation between economic freedom and happiness remains statistically significant. Unless we have a complex model that can separate the impact of all the different explanatory variables on each other, as well as on happiness, standard statistical techniques will seldom allow us to figure out which are the crucial variables explaining happiness.

[5] Veenhoven, *op. cit.* (2008).

The second problem arises because the number of possible determinants of happiness is considerably greater than the number of countries in the sample so that testing all these variables at the same time to determine the statistical significance of each is impossible. Cross-national comparisons of happiness have presented a wide variety of correlates of happiness, and there is no agreement about which are the most important. Examining this literature I found fifty-three possible determinants of happiness proposed by others that I felt deserved testing and that are listed and explained in greater detail in Appendix A-8. These include, for instance, motivation for achievement, belief in control over one's personal destiny, materialism, work values, subjective health ratings, fertility, and so forth. This heterogeneous (and seemingly strange, at first) list includes variables reflecting performance outcomes (social, economic, political, or health) and cultural conditions and attitudes. None of the fifty-three indicators is included in the variables that were previously used to define the economic system, so there is no overlapping that might bias the statistical results.

A simple solution for both of the problems noted above is to reduce the number of possible determinants through a principal component analysis. This statistical procedure, as briefly noted in Chapter 3, extracts the common explanatory factor (component) of a group of possible causal elements of happiness by means of a type of correlation analysis; the derived component will reflect their common impact on happiness. This component is then removed from possible causal elements and the process is repeated to derive a second component. Such a process can be repeated many times, although each derived component has decreasing explanatory value on happiness.

The first three principal components of these fifty-three possible determinants of happiness capture 54.1 percent of the total variation of their individual components. A key step in this calculation, presented in Appendix Table A-8, examines the correlation of these fifty-three possible determinants with the first three calculated principal components to ascertain the relative contribution to the component.

The first component reflects an effective and responsive government with a confident and individualistic population who trust each other; it is also the only component that, as I show below, is significantly related to happiness (with no other variables held constant). The second principal component is negatively related to happiness and reflects a population with relatively unequal incomes, high murder rates, high mortality, low marriage rates, and high religiousness(!). The third component is composed of quite different variables that do not easily lend themselves to a brief summary. The overall interpretation of all of these components of the determinants of happiness, however, is not important. What is crucial is that they isolate the common causal impact of their constituent determinants, so that we can determine the impact of the economic system.

C. Results

Using the results of the principal component analysis, we first calculate a score for each nation in the sample that shows how strongly its fifty-three characteristics reflect the composition of that particular component. The results of these calculations are presented in Appendix Table A-9. They indicate, for instance, that Sweden has the strongest relationship with the first principal component, while Greece has the weakest. If we hold these principal component scores constant, we have the necessary data to determine the impact of the economic system on happiness.

I conducted several rounds of statistical experiments with these data, and the final results are reported in Table 7–2.[6] These calculations allow us to focus directly

---

[6] In the first round of statistical experiments to explain the determinants of happiness, I included the logarithm of per capita GDP

Table 7-2. *Estimates Showing the Determinants of the Level of Happiness*

	Variable to be Explained: Average Level of Happiness of Each Nation							
	Scores for Each Country of the			Economic System Variable			
Constant	Principal Component 1 (effective, responsive government)	Principal Component 2 (unequal incomes, low social indicators)	Principal Component 3 (mixed indicators)	Mostly Anglo-Saxon	West European	South European	Adj R^2
7.199* (0.201)	0.028* (0.008)			-0.043 (0.207)	-0.022 (0.256)	0.195 (0.407)	.6042
7.711* (0.252)		0.013 (0.020)		-0.404 (0.342)	-0.543 (0.292)	1.120* (0.355)	.3100
7.530* (0.211)			-0.033 (0.021)	-0.141 (0.259)	-0.318 (0.297)	-0.978* (0.285)	.3824
6.973* (0.260)	0.031* (0.009)	-0.016 (0.016)	-0.026 (0.016)	0.256 (0.296)	0.221 (0.283)	0.477 (0.506)	.6382
7.214* (0.063)	0.024* (0.004)	-0.005 (0.010)	-0.025 (0.013)				.6818

Note: The equations calculated from the sample of twenty-one OECD nations should be read across the page. The calculated coefficients are shown in the first line of each pair of numbers; the standard errors are shown in parentheses and are used to determine the statistical significance of this coefficient, with an asterisk donating whether the coefficient meets this test. The economic systems are represented by 0–1 variables. The variable representing the *Nordic* economic system is used as the reference point, so the other economic system variables show the relationship with this economic system. The adj. R^2 is the adjusted coefficient of determination and denotes the percent of the variation (more technically, variance) of the level of happiness explained by the regression. The data for these regressions come from Tables 7–1 and Appendix Table A–9.

on one of the key questions motivating this chapter: does the economic system have an impact on subjective well-being? In the table, each of the economic systems is designated as either 0 or 1 (a dummy variable), with the *Nordic* economic system serving as the basis of comparison since this form of capitalism is associated with the highest average level of happiness. The other explanatory variables are the derived principal components combining the possible causal variables. Using a regression analysis we can hold these principal components constant to determine whether the individual economic systems have an impact on happiness.[7]

The first three regressions in the table show how happiness relates to each of the separate components and to 0–1 variables representing the different economic systems. The fourth regression, which presents the key results, includes the three components and the

in the various countries, even though some scholars have argued that for countries with a high per capita GDP, such as those in my sample, it should have little impact. Although per capita GDP is significantly related to happiness when examined in isolation, this correlation disappears when the various derived principal components are added to the calculated regression.

[7] Although there is a possibility of reverse causation with the three principal components (especially the second) and happiness, this should not bias the relationship between the economic systems variables and happiness.

three economic systems together; and the last regression includes just the derived components and to 0–1 variables representing the different economic systems. The fourth regression, which presents the key results, includes all of the three components and economic systems together; and the last regression includes just the derived components

For the equations including only one principal component and the economic system variables (the first three equations), the calculated results are meager and primarily show a significant difference in happiness only between the *Nordic* economic system (which serves as the comparison base) and *South European* economic system and only when the second and third principal components are held constant.

When the three components are included with the three economic system variables, none of the economic systems appears significantly different from the countries with a *Nordic* economic system, which have the highest average level of happiness (Table 7–1).[8] This is the

---

[8] In preliminary research, I examined the impact of several more components, but obtained the same negative results. I also carried out a similar analysis for the inequality of happiness and for the inequality-adjusted average level of happiness, but found nothing worth reporting.

regression that tells us clearly that the economic system has no significant relationship to happiness.

Although much more can be said about these results, one major result is clear: the economic system appears to play little role in the happiness of nations. Rather, it is the characteristics that compose the first principal component that account for the most important differences in happiness between nations.

D. Possible Objections

Statistical analysis thus appears to refute the ideological approach toward happiness: the population in allegedly gentle countries with a *Nordic* system and those allegedly "dog-eat-dog" nations with a *mostly Anglo-Saxon* system show no significant difference in average levels of happiness. But several possible objections can be immediately raised:

1. Disaggregation of Happiness Components
The calculated components of the determinants of happiness might be too aggregative, that is, they might mask the special impact of particular determinants that are crucial to happiness and that differ from one economic system to another. To explore this possibility, I separately tested the impact on happiness of each of the fifty-three

individual indicators used to calculate the various principal components.[9]

The results of this investigation can be quickly summarized: When these fifty-three indicators were individually held constant, not one of the economic systems variables had an impact on the average level of happiness.

2. Disaggregation of Systems Determinants

It can similarly be argued that particular institutions composing the economic systems might have an impact on happiness, so I calculated forty regression equations testing the impact on happiness of each of the forty institutions used to derive the economic system on the

---

[9] I calculated a set of 53 regressions of the following type:

$SWB = a + b_1 AS + b_2 WE + b_3 SE + d_1 PCS1 + d_2 PCS2 + d_3 PCS3 + e IDH$, SWB = subjective well-being; AS = dummy variable (a 0–1 variable) for *mostly Anglo-Saxon* nations, WE = dummy variable for *West European* nations, and SE = dummy variable for *South European* nations, with the *Nordic* countries providing the baseline; PCS1, PCS2, and PCS3 are the scores of the first three principal components; IDH = one of the 53 individual determinants contained in the principal components and listed in Appendix Table A-8;. The calculated regression coefficients are a,b,c,d, and e. In this regression the control variables are the component scores and the individual IDH's, and we are looking for any significant impact of the economic systems on happiness when the control variables are held constant.

happiness variable, holding the principal components constant. With one unimportant exception, when these individual institutions defining the economic system are added to the regression one at a time, none changed the conclusion that the economic system has no significant impact on happiness.[10]

---

[10] I calculated 40 regression of the following type:

$SWB = a + b_1 AS + b_2 WE + b_3 SE + d_1 PCS1 + d_2 PCS2 + d_3 OCS3 + e IIES$, where IIES = one of the 40 individual institutions composing the economic system. For the other variables, see the previous footnote. The one exception to the generalization in the text is that for the countries with a *South European* economic system, a higher concentration of corporate ownership led to greater happiness. The meaning of this single exception is unclear, and given the number of regressions that I ran, it could be a random result.

Objections can be raised to this procedure because if the economic systems are correlated with one or more of the three principal components of happiness, the results are biased. This can be easily tested by examining the correlation between the four individual economic systems and the three components of happiness. It turns out that eight of the twelve regressions show no significant relationships between economic system and the various components of happiness. In the other four cases, a correlation between the economic system and the principal component might have some impact on the results in Table 7–2, namely it might reduce the relationship between happiness with the economic system and its component variables. However, the correlation coefficients are low and this impact appears minor.

E. Interpretation of the Results

The data suggest that happiness is not related to the economic system, at least not in industrialized capitalist nations. But an important question remains: Why is the happiness of nations related to the political system but not the economic system?

One conjecture discussed at the beginning of the chapter is that individuals view the economic systems of their nations instrumentally, that is, their happiness depends on the performance results, rather than the system per se. People participate in the economy but not self-consciously in an economic system. Since, as noted in Chapter 6, the performance results of these four systems are roughly similar, we would not expect any difference in average happiness between economic systems. The data presented above support this conjecture.

By contrast, the results linking happiness to the political system suggest that self-conscious personal participation is an important characteristic of the political system, so that the form of the government does have an impact on happiness. In the economic system, people do not have the same feelings of self-conscious participation, that is, people shopping in the local mall do not constantly tell themselves that they are participants in a particular type of capitalist economy.

Happiness and Economic Systems

Three other possible reasons the economic system has so little apparent impact on average happiness deserve mention:

1. *Visibility.* The political system has a more immediate or visible impact on people's lives than the economic system, which is more abstract. In other words, people are more aware of the political system than the economic system and therefore are more likely to be psychologically affected by it. For instance, a referendum is an aspect of the political system in which people are directly aware of their role; it calls attention to the political system as such. In contrast, the economic system consists of many seemingly disparate institutions and is less apparently a system. Indeed, one major aim of this book is to make the economic system more visible to the reader.

2. *Helplessness.* People may feel that they have little power to change the economic system, unlike the political system, where they can use their right to vote for a change. The experience of voting and participating in activities intended to pressure the government for reform is direct and focused. The economic system is much harder to take on; only under revolutionary circumstances or during economic crises does it seem possible to change it through the actions of individuals. If the economic system is viewed as unalterable,

then people simply adapt to it and continue their lives. This parallels the finding discussed in the happiness literature, that paraplegics and others who have been seriously injured in accidents slowly adapt to their new circumstances and achieve in the long-term close to their previous level of happiness (although such long-run adjustment takes time and includes a period of intense unhappiness).[11]

3. *Basic similarity.* It is possible that although the OECD countries have different types of capitalisms, these systems are nevertheless sufficiently similar to create roughly equal levels of happiness. For instance, all are market economies with relatively free product, labor, land, and financial markets.

Detailed and comparable public opinion data with questions directed at these issues are not yet available. Although such information would take us further in understanding why the political system has an impact on subjective well-being, while the economic system does not, I strongly suspect that the conclusions reached in this chapter will not be greatly modified by the results of any such future research.

[11] This phenomenon is discussed by Philip Brickman, Dan Coates, and Ronnie Janoff-Bulman in "Lottery Winners and Accident Victims: Is Happiness Relative?" *Journal of Personality and Social Psychology* 36, no. 8 (1978): 917–27.

CHAPTER EIGHT

How Capitalism Will Change

Niels Bohr, the brilliant Nobel laureate in physics, once complained, "It is difficult to make predictions, especially about the future." Despite his warning, let's try. Even if we cannot know exactly how capitalism will change, we can, perhaps, detect some probable trends and directions.

Our first task is to survey some of the major forces that could lead to important institutional transformations. We then ask what types of general systemic change might result from such institutional transformations. Finally, we turn to existing capitalist systems and speculate briefly but with more specificity on how they might change in the next half-century.

A. Short-Run Factors Possibly Influencing Major Institutional and Systemic Change

Traumatic political/economic events are often a cause of major institutional change. For instance, Russia's defeat in the Crimean War (1854–56) set in motion forces that resulted in the abolition of serfdom five years later. The Great Depression of the 1930s led to greater state intervention into the economies of the OECD nations and much higher welfare transfers to the population. Less dramatically, British discontent with slow, uneven production growth in the post–World War II years appears to have played a major role in Margaret Thatcher's 1979 political victory and to have allowed her to make changes in the economic system, particularly the dismantling of governmental controls and detailed planning of the economy.

Will a transformation on the scale of what happened in the United Kingdom in the late 1970s again occur in the OECD nations as a result of the world economic crisis that took place at the end of the first decade of the twenty-first century? To provide some perspective on this question, Table 8–1 presents data on growth and fluctuations of aggregate production from 1975 through 2007 that supplements the data presented in Table 6–3.[1] While

[1] The data in Table 6–3 are, however, organized according to performance system, rather than economic system. That table also looks

Table 8–1. GDP Growth and Fluctuations in Industrial Capitalist Nations, 1975–2007[a]

Country	Average Annual GDP Growth	Fluctuation Measure	Country	Average Annual GDP Growth	Fluctuation Measure
A. Countries with a *mostly Anglo-Saxon* economic system			B. Countries with a *Nordic* economic system		
Australia	3.22%	2.35%	Denmark	2.14%	2.09%
Canada	2.78	2.84	Finland	2.50	5.19
Ireland	5.20	9.78	Norway	3.06	2.47
Japan	2.53	6.72	Sweden	2.07	3.54
New Zealand	2.25	5.33			
Switzerland?	1.64	2.20			
UK	2.42	3.85			
USA	3.06	2.12			
Average	2.89	4.27	Average	2.44	3.22
C. Nations with a *West European* economic system			D. Nations with a *South European* economic system		
Austria	2.35%	1.70%	Greece	2.05%	6.56%
Belgium	2.12	1.57	Italy	2.02	3.50
France	2.16	1.80	Portugal	2.94	4.38
Germany	2.13	3.13	Spain	2.82	3.87
Netherlands	2.58	3.03			
Average	2.27	2.25	Average	2.46	4.58

[a] The fluctuation measure is the average square of the deviation of each point from the ordinary least squares regression line used to determine the average annual GDP growth rate. It is also called the "mean square error." The GDP data come from the World Bank's *World Development Indicators* www.worldbank.org.

economic growth was certainly not dramatic in this period, which preceded the major economic crisis starting in 2007/2008, voters in the various countries did not appear to be sufficiently discontented with the economic system to force major changes, at least not at the time of writing. Equally important, none of the four capitalist economic systems in this period appears markedly superior in its macroeconomic performance. More specifically, the initial level of per capita GDP and the exposure to the outside world (measured in terms of the ratio of exports and imports to the GDP) are held constant, only the *mostly Anglo-Saxon* economic system had slightly (but statistically significant) higher growth rates than nations with the other systems; and only the nations with a *West European* economic system had a slightly lower (but statistically significant) rate of fluctuation of the GDP.[2]

    at growth of per capita GDP, while Table 8–1 focuses just on GDP growth.

[2] This calculation is similar to that shown in Table 6–3 but differs in that other possible causes of macroeconomic performance are held constant (namely, initial per capita GDP and openness of the economy). I also experimented with two other measures of fluctuations, the coefficient of determination of the GDP regressions and the average unemployment rate over the period. When other factors were held constant, neither of these two indicators revealed any statistically significant difference between the four economic systems.

In the recent global recession, measured from the 3d quarter of 2007 to the 3d quarter of 2009, the average annual decline in real GDP was 1.7 percent.[3] This decline, however, varied considerably among the OECD countries, with the countries with a Nordic economic system experiencing the greatest average fall in GDP; and the countries with a West European system, the least. Nevertheless, these differences were not statistically significant.

Such results, combined with those in Table 6–3, mean that no particular type of capitalism provided a clear model of emulation for the others, at least with regard to GDP growth.[4] Instead, the governments' policies and

---

[3] The data in this paragraph come from the OECD Web site www. OECD.org and were the last available at the time of writing.

[4] Of course, this doesn't necessarily mean that a greatly different economic system, such as central planning, would provide better results. For a comparison between economic performance of capitalist and centrally planned economies, see Frederic L. Pryor, *Economic Systems of Foraging, Agricultural, and Industrial Societies* (New York: Cambridge University Press, 2005). *op. cit.*; "Growth and Fluctuations of Production in OECD and East European Nations," *World Politics* 37, no. 2 (January 1985): 204–38; and "The Performance of Agricultural Production In Marxist and Non-Marxist Nations," *Comparative Economic Studies* 33, no. 3/1991: 95–127. These studies show that the centrally planned nations of Eastern Europe and the OECD nations of Western Europe did not have significantly different GDP growth rates and GDP fluctuations. For individual sectors, such as agriculture, the evidence is mixed and depends on the time period and the measure of fluctuations.

factors other than the economic system seemed to be the primary explanation for these different growth results. Consequently, unless the downturn in production in the industrial capitalist nations becomes considerably worse and lasts much longer lasting than it appeared in 2010, it seem unlikely that major systemic transformations will occur for two reasons: First of all, radical alternatives to capitalism, such as communist command systems, have been discredited; secondly, systemic inertia is formidable, as was shown in the Great Depression during the 1930s, when few countries adopted total different economic systems.

B. Long-Term Economic Trends Possibly Influencing Institutional Change

This section briefly outlines some challenging worldwide trends that are not easily met by existing institutions or current economic policies and that point to important institutional changes in the long-term future.

1. Demographic Changes

As everyone knows, the average age of the population in the OECD is rising. This will lead to a fall in the ratio of people in the traditional working ages (twenty through sixty-four) to people aged sixty-five and above.

For the OECD nations considered in this study, this ratio of working age to aged in 2000 averaged about 3.93; by 2040, it will be roughly 1.92.[5] In the latter year the ratio is predicted to be highest in nations with the *mostly Anglo-Saxon* and the *Nordic* economic systems and lowest in nations with the *West European* and *South European* economic systems, where predicted low birth rates will exacerbate the problem.

Obviously, the aging of the population will strain governmental pension and health care payments and old-age insurance. If current laws remain in force in the OECD, governmental expenditures for the aged as a ratio of the GDP are predicted to rise about twelve percentage points between 2000 and 2040, an increase which may be unsustainable.

2. Globalization

The word "globalization" has many meanings – political, legal, cultural, and economic. It also means that local events – phenomena as diverse as the incidence of disease and stock-market crashes – can have worldwide effects. The process of globalization also has many institutional impacts. For instance, enterprise governance,

---

[5] The data in this and the following paragraph come from Frederic L. Pryor, *Economic Systems of Foraging, Agricultural, and Industrial Societies, op. cit.*, Chapter 7.

which varies considerably between nations, even those with the same economic system, appears to be gradually converging, at least if we can believe the anecdotes in the business press. In this section, however, we focus only on several common indicators of globalization (foreign trade, market integration, immigration, and international flows of capital) to gain an overview of some quantitative measures of the process.

Foreign trade, as a share of total production of goods and services, rose almost twenty percentage points between 1952 and 2000 for the twenty-one OECD nations under consideration.[6] Market integration – the linking of markets for goods and services – is measured by price convergence in the OECD countries, and this gradually occurred, at least in the latter part of this period. Immigration rates rose dramatically in the last half of the twentieth century. More specifically, for the twenty-one OECD nations, the annual ratio of new immigrants to the total population rose from 0.2 to 0.8 percent between 1984 and 2000 (if illegal immigrants had been included, the increase would undoubtedly be higher). International capital (investment) flows have also soared: in the quarter century between 1972 and

---

[6] Data for the discussion in this paragraph come from the OECD and Frederic L. Pryor, *The Future of U.S. Capitalism* (New York: Cambridge University Press, 2002), Chapter 5.

1997, estimated world capital flows measured in constant prices, both direct (plant, equipment, and housing) and indirect (stocks and bonds) increased at an average annual rate of 8.3 percent, more than twice as fast as the growth of world GDP.

In the recession years between the third quarters of 2007 and 2009, the average annual decline in the dollar value of exports of the OECD countries of goods was 6.6 percent.[7] As in the case of the GDP, however, there was no significant difference in the countries with different economic systems.

Globalization also means that adverse economic shocks arising from the actions of other countries will have a greater impact on the domestic economy of each nation.[8] It will take years to strengthen institutions so as

[7] These data come from the OECD Web site www.OECD.com and were the latest available at the time of writing.

[8] One example of the international transmission of a local crisis: early in the twenty-first century a group of Wisconsin school boards borrowed money at a low interest rate from an Irish bank to purchase collateralized debt obligations (CDO) yielding a higher return. In 2008, when some of the underlying securities of the CDOs collapsed in value and the CDO issuers were unable to make their payments to the school districts, the latter could not then meet their interest payments on the loan from the Irish bank. This, in turn, placed the Irish bank in financial jeopardy, and, since it was owned by a German bank, the parent bank also found itself in a precarious financial position and had to be bailed out by the

to regulate international economic activities and prevent or mitigate worldwide shocks; meanwhile, we must rely on the informal coordination of policy actions in many countries, such as the G-20 group. In isolation, domestic actions to counter adverse macroeconomic events will become less effective. In a recession, for instance, the purchasing power arising from the increased governmental expenditures of a single nation will be partially spent abroad, so that fiscal policy becomes less effective. Other important implications of the globalization process, including income convergence or divergence between countries, must be left for others to discuss.

3. Increasing Scarcity of Natural Resources[9]

The world's total use of raw materials and foodstuffs has risen steeply in the past century because of the swelling population and increasing per capita production. Although global population growth has been slowing in the past few decades, the consumption of these basic products will undoubtedly continue to grow as per capita income increases and, other things being equal, will result

German government. There was no easy policy action that the German government could on its own have taken to have prevented this international transmission of a financial crisis.

[9] This discussion draws heavily upon the sources and analysis in Pryor, *The Future of U.S. Capitalism, op. cit.*, Chapter 6.

in supplies become increasingly strained. Nevertheless, this Malthusian nightmare of critical scarcities of foodstuffs and raw material and of their skyrocketing prices, did not come true in the twentieth century. It was kept at bay by technological progress in extracting, growing, refining, and processing these products, by the discovery of new mineral deposits, by the use of new land for agriculture, and by the production of new products that required fewer raw materials.

Unfortunately, it is unclear whether technology will continue to win the race with scarcity. In the first decade of the twenty-first century, the prices of many raw materials have risen much faster than the general price index. Moreover, as the long-term price of oil has climbed, the costs of some nonpetroleum sources of energy have increased as well. Given the stationary or declining oil production in most major oil-producing nations and the relatively few new discoveries of large oil deposits, it seems likely the long-term rising price of energy will continue until alternative energy sources become much more fully utilized.

Rising food prices seem likely as well: between 2000 and 2007 world food prices rose 80 percent, and many fear even steeper increases in the future. Probable underlying causes include global warming, water shortages, and the diversion of grains from food to the production of ethanol, which has, in turn, led to a reduction in the land used for other crops and feed for animals.[10]

If the relative prices of raw materials, energy, and foodstuffs rise, the low-income population will be the hardest hit, since raw-material intensive products and foods will cost more and thus constitute a higher share of the spending of this group. Thus, the distribution of real income will become more unequal. Moreover, the higher price of raw materials also means that for a given expenditure, fewer goods can be purchased, and for a given dollar of investment, less growth of goods and services will result.

4. Other Challenges

a. Savings and Growth. Where population is rising and where people spend down their wealth during retirement, the overall savings rate should decline under normal circumstances. as the number of workers per retirees declines. More specifically, empirical studies

---

[10] The datum on world food prices comes from Food and Agriculture Organization, "FAO Food Price Index," www.fao.org/worldfood-situation/FoodPriceIndex/en/ (accessed October 2008). In some countries, such as the United States, food prices increased only about 20 percent in the same period, which was roughly the same as the consumer price index.

show that a 1 percent rise in the ratio of the elderly to workers in the economy results in a decline in the ratio of savings to GDP of more than 0.3 percent.[11] Under even the most optimistic assumptions, the savings rate in the OECD countries in 2040 will be only slightly more than half the 2000 level (or even lower under more realistic assumptions). This means that economic growth of the OECD economies, in turn, will be considerably lower, other things being equal. Since economic growth often leads to higher employment and raises incomes of disadvantaged groups, the decline in economic growth will remove an important social lubricant. As a result, tensions between income groups may rise in the future. To avoid increased political repression, alternative institutions for alleviating such economic problems may have to be devised.

b. Microeconomic Volatility. Volatility can arise at the microeconomic level as well as the macroeconomic.

---

[11] The results of various empirical studies of the impact on savings of a rise in the elderly as a share of the population are summarized by Robert Stowe England in *The Macroeconomic Impact of Global Aging* (Washington, D.C.: Center for Strategic and International Studies, 2002). For a simulation model of the U.S. economy that takes these effects into account, see Frederic L. Pryor, "Demographic Effects on Personal Saving in the Future," *Southern Economic Journal* 69, no. 3 (January 2003): 541–60.

In the United States, for instance, certain microeconomic volatility measures have increased in the last third of a century, and a number of studies suggest that family incomes vary much more from year to year than they used to,[12] a phenomenon which puts affected families at greater risk. Risk has also risen for American families who find it hard to obtain affordable health insurance because of their preexisting health conditions or because their pensions are switching from defined-benefit to defined-contribution plans (such as 401 (k) plans).[13] This trend may, however, be modified by the health care bill signed into law in 2010, although, at the time of writing, it is difficult to know if this law will survive legal challenges. Of course, those living in capitalist countries with established universal health insurance or with predominantly defined-benefit pension plans do not face these

[12] Karen E. Dynan, Douglas W. Elmendorf, and Daniel E. Sichel, in "The Evolution of Household Income Volatility," *Finance and Economics Discussion* Series no. 61 (Washington, DC: Federal Reserve Board, 2007), present their estimates of this volatility and also provide an extremely useful survey of previous work on the topic by others.

[13] Peter Gosselin, in *High Wire: The Precarious Financial Lives of American Families* (New York: Basic Books, 2008), discusses a wide variety of other mounting financial risks faced by American families. Unfortunately, I have been unable to find comparable data for other OECD nations.

risks. Unfortunately, comparable long-term data on volatility of family incomes for other OECD countries are not available, but such data might reveal a similar increase in microeconomic volatility because foreign trade has a larger role in their economies.

c. Changing Relations Between Capital and Labor. Until recently, trends in the ownership and management of enterprises did not point toward dramatic institutional changes in production institutions.[14] During the financial crisis starting in 2007 and 2008, however, many governments bought shares in

[14] Three quite different indicators can be used to examine these issues: monopolization, as measured by the degree to which the top four or eight firms dominate the shipments of a narrowly defined industries; agglomeration, as measured by the share of total employment or industrial assets accounted for by the largest one hundred or one thousand firms; and the average size of enterprises, as measured by labor force or assets. Despite the growing number of mergers between enterprises, particularly in the 1990s, trends in these indicators in the latter part of the twentieth century give no cause for alarm and portend little dramatic change in the coming decades. In Pryor, *The Future of U.S. Capitalism, op. cit.* I discuss U.S. evidence on these matters; for Europe over a shorter time period, see Mikael Stenkula, "The European Size Distribution of Firms and Employment." Research Institute of Industrial Economics, IFN *Working Paper* no. 683 (Stockholm: RIIE, 2006).

enterprises – primarily banks, but in some cases producers as well – to provide them with liquidity and to prevent bankruptcy. At the time of writing, it is unclear whether such steps toward "socialism" will be reversed after the economy recovers or whether they represent a new direction and will be extended to other sectors of the economy. In brief, will the General Motors Corporation (GM), which was partially nationalized in 2009, be known in the future as "Government Motors?"

Labor markets may change as the labor force becomes more and more heterogeneous in terms of skills, ethnicity, and lifestyle. In most OECD nations, working-class solidarity appears to be declining, as manifested in a falling share of unionized workers in the labor force.[15] The weakening of labor unions has led to greater wage inequality and less job security, trends reinforced both by rising imports of labor-intensive goods from developing countries that pay much lower wages and by an increased willingness by employers in many countries to use wage

---

[15] Several of the *Nordic* countries are exceptions to this generalization. Underlying data are provided by Miriam Golden, et al., "Postwar Trade-Union Organization and Industrial Relations in Twelve Countries," pp. 194–230 in Herbert Kitschelt et al., eds., *Continuity and Change in Contemporary Capitalism* (New York: Cambridge University Press, 1999); and Jelle Visser, "Union Membership Statistics in roughly 24 Countries," *Monthly Labor Review* 129, no. 1 (January 2006): 38–49.

differentials as part of incentive packages to encourage more work from their employees. These trends reinforce the growing income inequality arising from higher relative prices of foodstuffs and raw materials.

C. Types of Systemic Change

In Chapter 4, we delineated four distinct economic systems of advanced capitalist nation, defined in terms of clusters of complementary institutions. This result suggests a certain "logic of institutions." That is, an economic institution cannot be wildly out of sync with all the other institutions in the economic system. Thus, as a system changes, all of its institutions must change in a related fashion at roughly the same time. An empirical demonstration of this concept using the various institutional characteristics presented in *Economic Freedom of the World* shows that institutions and policies associated with different facets of economic freedom change together both over time and also across countries at the same time.[16]

---

[16] The calculation is carried out by Russell S. Sobel and Christopher J. Coyne in "Cointegrating Institutions: The Time-Series Properties of Country Institutional Measures," submitted for publication, 2010. Their data on institutions come from James D. Gwartney and Robert A. Lawson, *Economic Freedom of the World* (Vancouver: Fraser Institute, 2008).

Three critical questions arise from such considerations: If institutional changes occur in OECD countries, will the same countries remain in the same economic system, that is, will they still cluster together? Will nations with the same economic system become even more similar? And will the different economic systems tend to converge?

These questions concern complex changes over time, and an empirical study to answer them by delineating economic systems in past years is difficult to carry out because we have few quantitative measures of institutions before 1990 – in fact, I could locate only eleven. Although we cannot hope for conclusive answers, we can obtain some tentative and tantalizing results.

1. Parallel versus Random Systemic Change

The "logic of institutions" suggests two types of parallel change to investigate. The first is *parallel institutional change*, which occurs when the clustering of countries in economic systems remains the same, even though the individual institutional components of these systems (or the measures of these institutions) have changed in value. For instance, over a given period, the ratio of public expenditures to GDP in the *West European* countries can always be higher than that in the *mostly Anglo-Saxon* group of nations, even though the values of these ratios vary considerably at different points in time. These parallel changes can be contrasted with random institutional change, which occurs when changes in the institutional indicators follow a haphazard pattern and are quite different among countries that formerly had the same economic system.

Did the OECD nations manifest parallel or random institutional changes? Since these nations had largely recovered from the effects of World War II by the end of the 1950s, I start the analysis with data for four benchmark years thereafter, namely 1960, 1970, 1980, and 1990, and then determine the rank orderings of the average values of the four economic systems for each of the eleven institutional indicators in the benchmark years.

The test results are clean. For ten out of the eleven institutional indicators, the rank orderings of the averages of the four economic systems were the same in all four years. In sum, the OECD nations have exhibited parallel institutional change. Nevertheless, important changes in the values of these indicators occurred. For instance, the ratio of public consumption to total (public plus private) consumption in the *Nordic* nations was roughly the same as the OECD average in the early 1950s, but it had moved ahead of all other OECD systems by 1960, and in the following years this gap widened even more. Thus, a distinctive characteristic of the current *Nordic* economic system – their welfare state – began to emerge only in the mid-1950s, even though the ideological seeds may have been planted decades earlier.

One immediate objection to this analysis of parallel institutional change can be raised. The comparisons involved cover only thirty years, and the relationships might not hold over a longer period. For instance, data on public expenditures extending back to 1870 show sharp breaks in the rank ordering of nations before and after World War II.[17] Similarly, with regard to the openness of foreign trade, as measured by average tariff rates, the rank orderings of the four groups of nations greatly changed over the last 120 years, showing sharp breaks after both world wars.[18] This indicates that the logic of

[17] The underlying data come from Thomas R. Cusack and Susanne Fuchs, "Parteien, Institutionen und Staatsausgaben." In Herbert Obinger, et al., eds., *Politische Ökonomie: Politik und wirtschaftliche Leistungsprofile in OECD Demokratien* (Opladen: Leske und Büdrich, 2003), 321–54 However, I have had to make a number of estimates to extend some of the series back to 1870. Peter H. Lindert, *Growing Public: Social Spending and Economic Growth since the Eighteenth Century* (New York: Cambridge University Press, 2004), shows that many of the differences in the rank orderings among nations can be traced to changes in the extent of the voting franchise and the degree of democracy.

[18] The graph of the degree of trade openness over time is complex. Tariff rates in a worldwide sample of thirty-five nations slowly rose from the 1870s to the first decade of the twentieth century,

institutions is a phenomenon primarily relevant just in the short and medium runs. Of course, this makes long-run prediction of changes in economic systems more difficult.

The second type of parallel change is *parallel country change*, which occurs when countries with the same economic system remain clustered together at different points in time when all institutions are taken into account, even as the pattern of their complementary institutions changes. In contrast, random country changes occur when countries that clustered together in one period cease to do so later. This happens when countries

then rose dramatically from the 1920s to the late 1930s, so that at their peak they were roughly twice as high as the late-nineteenth-century average, and then slowly declined from the late 1940s to the 1990s. See Christopher Blattman, Michael A. Clements, and Jeffrey G. Williamson, "Who Protected and Why? Tariffs the World Around 1870–1938," Harvard Institute of Economic Research *Discussion Paper* no. 2010 (Cambridge, MA: HIER, 2003). During these three periods, the relative position of countries changed considerably. For instance, the U.S. was a high-tariff nation in the late-nineteenth century, but in the interwar period (up to the enactment of the Smoot-Hawley tariff bill in the early 1930s) had relatively low tariffs, compared both to previous eras and contemporary rates in other countries. Obviously certain changes in the external international economic environment have also been important, such as the influence after World War II of the GATT treaty (General Agreement on Trade and Tariffs) and the creation of the European common market.

in one system that had higher quantitative measures for particular institutions than those of another system no longer manifest such differences in the next period.

To examine parallel country changes, I employ a cluster analysis to determine the economic systems in each of the four years under investigation. Unfortunately, the eleven indicators available for the historical analysis are not necessarily representative of the entire economic system.[19] In fact, for the overlap year 1990, an eleven-indicator comparison placed only three-quarters of the countries in the same clusters into which they fell when a forty-indicator comparison was used. In the 1960–1980 period, between 48 and 57 percent of the countries were found in the same clusters to which the forty-indicator analysis for 1990 had allotted them.

These results are not conclusive, and three interpretations can be offered: (1) *parallel country change* occurs, but it is not very strong; (2) the eleven indicators are really not representative of all the key economic institutions; or (3) economic systems are mutable over time. Case-study materials can provide some clues, so let us focus on the case of the United Kingdom in the postwar period, a

---

[19] This discussion draws upon evidence presented in Frederic L. Pryor, *Economic Systems of Foraging, Agricultural, and Industrial Societies, op. cit.,* Chapter 7.

well-known example of a country experiencing considerable systemic change.

In a survey of a group of specialists in economic systems, a majority rated Great Britain in the early 1960s as having more national planning and government direction of the economy than most other OECD nations.[20] My own cluster analysis using eleven institutional indicators placed the United Kingdom in the *West European* system in 1960 and not the *mostly Anglo-Saxon* system, which has had a more laissez-faire economic system. For the late 1990s, a much more systematic study, using both a survey of laws and observer opinions, put the United Kingdom among those OECD nations with the least governmental participation in the economy.[21] Correspondingly, my own analysis of the same eleven indicators in 1990 also placed the United Kingdom among those with a *mostly Anglo-Saxon* economic system. In brief, over the thirty years from 1960 to 1990, the capitalist economic system of the United Kingdom had greatly changed.

The high degree of government intervention in the U.K. economy in the 1950s and early 1960s might be

---

[20] Myron H. Ross, "Fluctuations in Economic Activity," *American Economic Review* 55, no. 1 (March 1965): 158–61.

[21] Giuseppe Nicoletti and Frederic L. Pryor, "Subjective and Objective Measures of the Extent of Government Regulation," *Journal of Economic Behavior and Organization* 59, no. 3 (2005): 433–49.

attributed to the self-reinforcing process of a slow wartime recovery and inertia in removing inappropriate
wartime controls of the economy. But disappointing
economic performance in the first three decades following World War II resulted in a shift in the balance of
political forces and, most likely, in ideology as well. In
analyzing the U.K.'s economic system, most commentators have focused on the 1979 election of Margaret
Thatcher, whose government sold off state enterprises,
reduced labor unions' influence in national economic
policy making, and, as briefly noted above, cut back the
governments' other roles in the economy. In 1990, her
last year in office, the economic system of the United
Kingdom had become like that of other nations in the
mostly Anglo-Saxon group. But if we look at the eleven historical indicators discussed above, this process appears to
have begun in the mid-1970s: Thatcher's policies appear,
in part, as the culmination of a previous trend.

The lesson from this example is that a country can
change its economic system, even if the changes in particular institutions are not well synchronized with other
institutions. This requires, however, that the political
leadership be tough and strong, follow consistent policies, and be able to maintain enough political support
for a sufficiently long period to overcome the resistance
arising from the pain that such policies inflict because of

the inconsistencies between institutions that have and have not been yet changed.

One can carry out other tests of parallel country changes, but the results come as no surprise.[22] The results above, however, show that parallel institutional change appears to be much stronger than parallel country change. Both types of change also provide support for the logic-of-institutions approach, at least in the short and middle runs.

2. Converging or Diverging Systemic Changes

Do economic systems tend to become more or less similar to each other over time? We can explore this long-term issue by first carrying out a cluster analysis of institutions in developing economies, using virtually the same institutional indicators as for the OECD nations. Then by comparing the average differences between the clusters in the two set of countries, as well as the degree to which these clusters explain the differences between nations with the same economic system, we can gain some idea about systemic changes over time.[23]

---

[22] Most importantly, these tests included a concordance analysis of the rank orders of countries.

[23] Frederic L. Pryor, "Economic Systems of Developing Nations," *Comparative Economic Studies* 48, no. 1 (March 2006): 77–98. The comparisons between the sample of OECD and developing

The results can be quickly summarized: the clusters of the developing economies are further apart from each other than the OECD countries; moreover, the differences between same-system nations are greater in the former than the latter group of nations, that is, the individual clusters cover a much larger institutional space among the developing countries. In brief, both between-system and within-system distances are greater in the developing economies. This appears reasonable if we consider the much-different starting points at which the developing economies began to enter the modern age and the hypothesis, oft-expressed by modernization theorists, that industrial economies impose more constraints on economic operations than agricultural economies do. Agricultural economies are much less complex and have many fewer institutional interconnections.

When a similar test is carried out for the OECD nations with just the eleven available institutional indicators for 1960 through 1990, no apparent trends can be found in the between-cluster and within-cluster distances. Again, however, we are faced with a problem of interpretation: Are we getting these results because the eleven-institution sample is not representative, because

economies are made in Pryor, *Economic Systems of Foraging, Agricultural, and Industrial Societies, op. cit.,* Chapter 7.

the time period is too short, or because convergence is solely a long-term phenomenon?

3. Speed of Change

Institutions can seem frozen in time. For instance, in the OECD nations, the measures of the central bank's policy independence from the Ministry of Finance showed little variation from the 1950s to the 1990s, that is, until the establishment of the European Central Bank. The most noticeable exception was the increasing policy independence of the *South European* central banks, which went from well below the OECD average in 1951 to about average in 1990.

In other cases, institutional changes were slow but apparent, and in one direction. For example, in the OECD economies governmental expenditures (both consumption and transfers) as a ratio of GDP rose steadily over this period from 26.3 percent in 1952 to 44.5 percent in 1990. Similarly, indicators of other institutions, such as worker protection against job loss and openness of trade in goods, services, and capital, also showed a steady increase over time.

In still other cases, institutional changes have been reversed: that is, the system changed in the short run but not in the long run. For instance, in the year immediately following the end of World War II, there was a strong wave of nationalization of industry in most OECD nations. In the ensuing four decades, however, public ownership of the means of production declined in most of these same nations.[24] As noted above, government ownership also increased during the financial crisis that started in late 2007, and this institutional change may (or may not) be temporary. Other cases of the rise and fall of particular institutions are more difficult to characterize.[25]

Finally, systemic change can sometimes occur quite rapidly. Military occupation and/or a political revolution can result in a dramatic and rapid overhaul of the economic system, as was seen in the first decade after World War II in Central and Eastern Europe. In these countries, the imposition of a new economic system, communism, was bloody and repressive. Rapid systemic change again

---

[24] Piet Angelo Toninelli, *The Rise and Fall of State-Owned Enterprise in the Western World* (New York: Cambridge University Press, 2000).

[25] For instance, it is sometimes argued that corporatist institutions reveal a similar rise and fall. Certainly, some trappings of corporatism disappeared in some European countries after the mid-1970s, following the oil shock and subsequent economic difficulties. Nevertheless, according to the research I reported in "Corporatism as an Economic System," *Journal of Comparative Economics* 12, no. 3 (September 1988): 317–44, the tide of corporatism was not ebbing in the OECD as a whole, at least up to 1990, even though such a trend is found in some OECD countries.

occurred in this region from the early 1990s to the early 2000s after the fall of communism; and, while it was not bloody, it, too, was painful for large portions of the population.[26] Rapid systemic changes can also be triggered, as noted above, from defeat in warfare or a disastrous economic crisis.

For the industrial OECD nations, rapid systemic change seems unlikely in the foreseeable future. As one may infer from the previous discussion, there are few indicators (except for, possibly, the nationalization of industry) that we will see major shifts toward one particular type of capitalism rather than another. Furthermore, parallel country change seems likely to persist: in the near future the grouping of nations into particular economic systems will probably be quite similar to what it is today, as will the relative degree to which certain institutions are manifest in the various countries.

On the other hand, it also seems highly likely that the capitalist economic systems of industrial nations will gradually converge in the very long run. First, most of these nations belong to the European Union, which is trying to harmonize the business practices and laws of its member nations. Second, all of the nations belong to

[26] See Anders Åslund, *How Capitalism Was Built: The Transformation of Central and Eastern Europe, Russia, and Central Europe* (New York, NY : Cambridge University Press, 2007).

certain international organizations, such as the Bank for International Settlements in Basel or the World Intellectual Property Organization in Geneva, which are likewise aiming for uniformity. Third, between the early 1950s and 2000, differences in the level of economic development (measured by per capita GDPs) of the various nations narrowed considerably, and this trend seems likely to continue in the future.[27]

D. Future Systemic Change in the OECD Nations

Having looked briefly at the types and processes of systemic change, we might try to speculate on exactly how these economic systems will be different in the far future. But while the discussion up to now of parallel institutional and systemic change, systemic convergence, and speed of systemic change may vary in the future, these concepts do not help very much in predicting particular changes in individual systems.

However, several ways to analyze future systemic changes are still open to us. Since we used forty indicators of economic institutions to define the four economic

[27] The data underlying this statement come from Angus Maddison, *The World Economy* (Paris: OECD, 2003).

systems of the industrial OECD nations, we could examine how the forces underlying institutional change will impact each of the indicators. A less tedious method is to explore the most probable changes in what I believe to be the institutions most likely to experience important transformations. These changes mostly refer to industrial capitalist countries in general; only a country-by-country survey of laws and institutions can reveal which economic systems will be most affected.

1. Financial Sector

As indicated in Chapter 6, the world economic crisis starting in 2007/2008 was primarily triggered by events in the financial sector. If governments wish to avoid similar downturns in the future, the financial sector must experience important institutional and policy changes in the years to come. It is unclear, however, how large these changes will be, given the array of powerful political forces opposing any major modifications. Change might be confined primarily to regulation procedures, or it might go further and alter the structure of other sectors as well.

Regarding bank regulation, a recent IMF analysis of commercial bank performance in eleven OECD nations showed clearly that governmental regulation of bank liquidity and of the relative roles of bank-asset funding from deposits and from borrowing, significantly affected bank performance and failures in late 2007.[28] This suggests that if the regulatory regime is improved, major structural reforms may not be necessary in some countries.

Markets for various exotic derivatives, sub-prime mortgages, collateralized debt obligations, credit default options, and similar financial instruments will undoubtedly be more constrained in the future.[29] For instance, banks bundling many mortgages into a new securities may be required to retain a certain percentage of these

[28] Lev Ratnovski and Rocco Huang. "Why Are Canadian Banks More Resilient?" IMF *Working Paper* WP/09/152 (Washington, D.C.: International Monetary Fund, 2009). Another study by Andrea Beltratti and René Stulz, "Why Did Some Banks Perform Better During the Credit Crisis? A Cross-Country Study of the Impact of Governance and Regulation," The National Bureau of Economic Research *Working Paper* 15180 (Cambridge, MA: NBER, 2009) also shows the importance of certain regulatory policies, although it places more emphasis on bank governance as a factor of bank performance during the crisis period from 2007 up to 2009.

[29] It is noteworthy that Africa, where most countries limit the types of activities in which financial institutions can engage, was the only continent untouched by the recent financial crisis (at least up to the time of writing). This suggests one useful way in which the more "advanced" countries might change their economic systems.

new securities, so that they will bear part of the risk of default and, thus, will be more conscious of the risks they are passing on to others. This percentage might also be adjustable by the central bank, just as some central banks can adjust the margin for individuals buying securities on credit. In addition, certain banking practices, such as "liar loans" (loans given with no investigation of the borrowers' stated income or ability to repay) (these were also called NINJA loans, indicating that borrowers had no income, no job, and no assets), or the sale of high-interest (sub-prime) mortgages to those with little ability to pay them off might be similarly restricted. Stricter controls may also be placed on the activities of hedge funds and other firms leveraging their capital by borrowing at low interest rates to speculate on allegedly high-yielding assets. It also seems likely that the degree of financial leveraging by banks, "nonbank banks," hedge funds, and the like, will also be further restricted. In brief, we can probably expect constraints on a great many financial activities, businesses, and individuals that heretofore have received little governmental pressure to reduce financial leveraging. Whether these measures will be sufficient to avoid the kind of economic shocks recently experienced by the world's financial sector remains to be seen.

Structural transformations of the financial sector, originating either internally or in response to government actions, may also take place in some countries. An important transformation occurring during the financial crisis that began in late 2007 was the considerable consolidation of banks in some OECD nations, as strong banks purchased weaker ones to save them either from illiquidity or bankruptcy. At that time, this trend did not cause great alarm since some econometric evidence suggests that countries with more concentrated banking structures are less likely to experience banking crises.[30] Nevertheless, increasing concentration of the financial sector can, in some cases, lead to increasing concentration of investment or production, which has negative consequences. The growing importance of sovereign wealth funds (investment funds controlled by governmental agencies) in certain nations with large deposits of raw materials and oil tends also to promote centralization of the financial sector. Although governmental actions can limit concentration of the financial sector, it is unclear whether these steps will be taken.

2. Government Sector

In major respects, the power of governments to influence aggregate economic activities will become weaker.

---

[30] Thorsten Beck, Asli Demirgüç-Kunta, and Ross Levine, "Bank Concentration, Competition, and Crises: First Results," *Journal of Banking and Finance* 30, no. 5 (2006): 1581–1603, presents evidence for this claim.

Such a process can already be seen in federal countries, such as the United States or Germany, where the subordinate governmental units (for instance, the states of the United States, Länder in Germany) have little impact on macroeconomic aggregates in their areas of jurisdiction. Moreover, as we saw earlier, increasing globalization will probably lead to greater aggregate volatility since globalization makes nations more vulnerable to economic shocks originating abroad. At the same time, moreover, the national governments will have fewer macroeconomic tools with which to offset cyclical swings because the increased volume of imports will diminish the impact of governmental intervention. That is, more of the new purchasing power (money) pumped into the economy by the government to offset declines in consumption will go abroad rather than circulate internally. Similarly, attempts by governments to stimulate investment by lowering interest rates may speed up the outflow of investment funds to countries with higher interest rates. The governments of the European OECD nations have essentially handed over their monetary power to the European Central Bank, which may not be willing to take interest rate actions that would affect all countries in the monetary union just to assist a few distressed countries.

Globalization will lead to a similar weakening of regulatory powers, as countries are forced to coordinate their microeconomic policies – either through a supranational organization, treaties, or by very frequent contact. National regulations are also enfeebled by the increasing importance of services, which are difficult to control because of their heterogeneity and complexity. For instance, a contributing cause of the 2007/2008 financial crisis was the sale of derivative securities by financial companies. These securities were so complex that few people – including the professional rating agencies – were able (or willing) to assess their risks. In the United States, the institutions selling such securities did not care about the risk as long as it could be passed on to others, and when the liabilities could not be paid off, a chain reaction of bankruptcies began.

But just as governments find themselves less able to control the economy, citizens will be expecting them to do more: they will demand governmental actions that protect family income from the greater volatility accompanying globalization, especially since individuals can not easily take countermeasures by themselves. Such governmental policies would include both direct transfer payments and various indirect actions such as greater regulation of private pensions and more constraints on markets for consumer goods and services. Many of these measures, which have been in place in the *Nordic* countries, will have to be introduced in some of the other economic systems as well.

During the global recession starting in late 2007, the share of public expenditures in the GDP rose to stimulate the economy by providing additional purchasing power, to bail out various financial enterprises and other enterprises, and to pay for greater welfare expenditures. How long these additional expenditures will last is, at the time of writing, unknown. However, it seems certain that the share of public expenditures in the GDP will rise in the future, driven by the rising ratio of the elderly to those in the working cohorts and by the rising costs of medical care as increasingly expensive cures are brought on line. Of course, countermeasures could be taken: raising the retirement age and/or the age at which pensions from the social insurance system are received; reducing the per capita amount of these payments; rationing the medical services financed by the government; or cutting back on other government expenditures, such as education, defense, agriculture, or economic regulation. Politically, however, these steps are very difficult to take and elected governments propose or implement such measures only at their peril.

3. The Labor Sector
The political and economic power of workers seems to be trending downward in most OECD nations. The share of union workers has fallen in most countries, a trend that is likely to continue as service workers become an

ever-rising share of the labor force. In some – but not all – OECD nations, this weakening of workers' power can also be seen in the declining share of labor income in the national income (after removing the labor income of corporate officers)[31] and a widening wage inequality, abetted by an ever-increasing downward pressure on the wages of low-skilled workers as labor-intensive imports from developing countries that pay their workers lower wages enter the market.

As noted above, the aging of the population in the OECD nations will result in less net saving and lower economic growth. This may well exacerbate the social tensions arising from widening income inequalities because countries will be less able to alleviate poverty through economic growth alone. A fraying of the social fabric may also result from the growing heterogeneity of the population that is brought on by immigration. For instance, studies show that democratic governments in areas with more heterogeneous populations spend less on social services and education. On the other hand, alienation from the government, as manifested by such indicators as the willingness of people to cheat on their taxes, does not seem to have changed very much for

---

[31] For the United States, relevant data are provided and analyzed by Philip Jefferson and Frederic L. Pryor, "Dynamics of U.S. Factor Income Shares," *Journal of Income Distribution*, 19, no. 1 (March 2010).

the OECD as a whole, at least in the 1990s.[32] Again, we face the problem that we can identify general systemic changes without being able to determine exactly how individual systems will change.

4. A Brief Summary

The discussion up to now has provided a general flavor of possible future changes in the economic system. Each nation or economic system has its peculiar circumstances, of course, and predicting the individual trajectories of each is beyond the scope of this the present survey. Therefore, discussion in this chapter has focused on the direction of general changes in institutions rather than to specific changes in particular countries or systems.

While we can point to imperfections in current institutions that compose the economic system and speculate on how they can be improved, it is much more difficult to determine how any changes taken will fit together, especially since modifications in one institution may

---

[32] Ronald Inglehart et al., *Human Beliefs and Values* (Mexico City: Siglo XXI Editores, 2004), present survey data for many nations on responses to the question of whether it is justifiable to cheat on one(s taxes if one has a chance (question F116). For the OECD nations between 1990 and 2000, no significant change in responses occurred, even when per capita GDP and economic system are held constant.

influence the performance of another. For instance, alterations in the financial system may lead to less investment and economic growth, which, in turn, can affect the operation of the labor market. Thus, gaining insight into the operation of the entire system, which embraces many different but interconnected, institutions, is a particularly difficult task.

Recent election campaigning in various OECD nations leads to the unfortunate conclusion that few politicians have a sufficiently consistent vision of the future economic system to make wise policy decisions or to implement a consistent program for changing the economic system.

E. Parting Words

This short book has covered a great deal of territory. We have seen why capitalism emerged in northwestern Europe in the nineteenth century rather than in other parts of the world. There were a variety of enabling factors in Northwestern Europe, including a higher level of economic development, a system of law and order that more or less prevailed, protection of private property, the existence of institutions that helped to spread new technological knowledge, and national governments that generally provided the necessary roads and other overhead capital but did not greatly interfere in production. Among the current industrialized nations of the OECD, we saw how the configurations of economic institutions lead us to delineate four economic systems.

The economic and social/economic performance indicators of the OECD countries in the sample fall into the same distinct country groups as the countries in the economic and social systems. Although these economic systems do not greatly differ in their performance, they do show considerable differences in their social/economic outcomes. In the economic sphere, for instance, although the *mostly Anglo-Saxon* nations have significant investment efficiency (that is, higher output per unit of additional investment), but also greater income inequality at high incomes and higher levels of air pollution, they do not significantly differ in most other performance measures. In a given economic system, countries that score higher for a one set of performance indicators may score lower than countries than other economic systems for a different set of indicators, so that a trade-off of performance variables seems to occur. We could not, however, find any evidence that any of these economic systems produced happier people.

Barring cataclysmic economic events, we can expect current OECD economic systems to evolve slowly and in a piecemeal fashion, with changes in a few institutions occurring in one period, followed in subsequent periods by adjustments in other institutions. Although it is difficult to make predictions, I have tried to point to those areas in which system change is most likely to occur in the fields of finance, government, and labor.

This reassessment of capitalism allows us to reconsider the big questions about our economic system: What is capitalism? How does it usually perform? Where is the system going, and do we need to change it totally to avoid a repetition of our current economic difficulties? I hope that I have provided a new perspective from which to address these questions. It is my hope that this book has provided fresh insights into capitalism and on some potential changes to this system that may happen in the future.

Bibliography

Including sources cited in the appendices on the web.

Adelman, Irma, and Cynthia Taft Morris. "Patterns of Market Expansion in the Nineteenth Century: A Quantitative Study." In George Dalton, ed. *Research in Economic Anthropology*. Vol. 1, pp. 231–325. Greenwich, CT: JAI Press, 1978.

Akerlof, George A., and Robert J. Shiller. *Animal Spirits: How Human Psychology Drives the Economy and Why It Matters for Global Capitalism*. Princeton, NJ: Princeton University Press, 2009.

Alesina, Alberto, Arnaud Devleeschauwer, William Easterly, Sergio Kurlat, and Romain Wacziarg. "Fractionalization." *Journal of Economic Growth* 8, no. 2 (2003): 155–94.

Allen, Robert C., Jean-Pascal Bassino, Debin Ma, Christine Moll-Murata, and Jan Luiten van Zanden. "Wages, Prices, and Living Standards in China." 2005. http://www.iisg.nl/hpw/papers/allen–et–al.pdf.

Amable, Bruno. *The Diversity of Modern Capitalism*. Oxford: Oxford University Press, 2003.

Bibliography

Åslund, Anders. *How Capitalism Was Built: The Transformation of Central and Eastern Europe, Russia, and Central Europe.* New York: Cambridge University Press, 2007.

Aston, Trevor Henry, and C. H. E. Philpin, eds. *The Brenner Debate: Agrarian Class Structure and Economic Development in Pre-Industrial Europe.* New York: Cambridge University Press, 1985.

Bäckman, Olof. "Institutions, Structures and Poverty: A Comparative Study of 16 Countries, 1980–2000," *European Sociological Review* 25, no. 2 (2009): 251–64.

Baechler, Jean, John A. Hall, and Michael Mann, eds. *Europe and the Rise of Capitalism.* New York: Blackwell, 1988.

Bairoch, Paul. "The Main Trends in National Economic Disparities since the Industrial Revolution." In Paul Bairoch and Maurice Levy-Leboyer, eds. *Disparities in Economic Development since the Industrial Revolution*, pp. 3–17. New York: St. Martin's Press, 1975.

"Écarts internationaux des niveaux de vie avant la révolution industrielle," *Annales: Économies, Sociétés, Civilisations* 34, no. 1 (January 1979): 145–72.

Cities and Economic Development: From the Dawn of History to the Present. Translated by Christopher Braider. Chicago: University of Chicago Press, 1988.

Barbera, Robert J. *The Cost of Capitalism.* New York: McGraw Hill, 2009.

Barrett, David B., ed. *World Christian Encyclopedia.* New York: Oxford University Press, 1982.

Barth, Erling, and Karl O. Moene. "The Equality Multiplier," *National Bureau of Economic Research Working Paper* No. 15076. Cambridge, MA, NBER, 2009.

Beach, William W., and Tim Kane. "Methodology: Measuring the 10 Economic Freedoms." 2008. http://www.heritage.org/Index.

Bibliography

Beck, Thorsten, Asli Demirgüç–Kunta, and Ross Levine. "Bank Concentration, Competition, and Crises: First Results." *Journal of Banking & Finance* 30, no. 5 (2006): 1581–1603.

Beltratti, Andrea, and René M. Stulz. "Why Did Some Banks Perform Better During the Credit Crisis? A Cross-Country Study of the Impact of Governance on Regulation." *National Bureau of Economic Research Working Paper* No. 15180. Cambridge, MA: NBER, 2009.

Berger, Peter L. *The Capitalist Revolution.* New York: Basic Books, 1986.

Berman, Harold J. *Law and Revolution: The Formation of the Western Legal Tradition.* Cambridge, MA: Harvard University Press, 1983.

Bernhardt, Kathryn, and Philip C. C. Huang, eds. *Civil Law in Qing and Republican China.* Stanford, CA: Stanford University Press, 1994.

Blaiklock, Alison J., et al. "When the Invisible Hand Rocks the Cradle." Innocenti Working Papers No. 93 (2002). http://www.unicef-icdc.org/publications/pdf/iwp93.pdf.

Blattman, Christopher, Michael A. Clemens, and Jeffrey G. Williamson. "Who Protected and Why? Tariffs the World Around, 1870–1938." Harvard Institute of Economic Research Discussion Paper No. 2010. Cambridge, MA: HIER, 2003.

Bowles, Samuel. "Endogenous Preferences: The Cultural Consequences of Markets and Other Economic Institutions." *Journal of Economic Literature* 36, no. 1 (1998): 75–111.

Brandolini, Andrea, and Timothy M. Smeeding. "Inequality: International Evidence." n.d. http://www.unicatt.it/Dottorati/Defap/Allegati/Inequality_international_evidence.pdf.

Bibliography

Braudel, Fernand. *Civilization and Capitalism, 15th–18th Century. Vol. 3. The Perspective of the World*. Translated by Siân Reynolds. New York: Harper & Row, 1984 [orig. 1979].

Brenner, Robert. "Agrarian Class Structure and Economic Development in Pre-Industrial Europe." 1985. In Aston and Philpin, eds., pp. 10–63.

Brickman, Philip, Dan Coates, and Ronnie Janoff-Bullman. "Lottery Winners and Accident Victims: Is Happiness Relative?" *Journal of Personality and Social Psychology* 36, no. 8 (1978): 917–27.

Centre national de la recherche scientifique. *Trésor de la langue française*. Paris: CNRS, 1977.

Cipolla, Carlo M. *Literacy and Development in the West*. Hammondsworth, U.K.: Penguin, 1969.

Corning, Peter A. *Holistic Darwinism: Synergy, Cybernetics, and the Bioeconomics of Evolution*. Chicago: University of Chicago Press, 2005.

Croot, Patricia, and David Parker. "Agrarian Class Structure and the Development of Capitalism: France and England Compared." In Aston and Philpin, eds., pp. 79–91.

Cusack, Thomas R., and Susanne Fuchs. "Parteien, Institutionen und Staatsausgaben." In Herbert Obinger, Uwe Wagshal, and Berhard Kittel, eds. *Politische Ökonomie: Politik und wirtschaftliche Leistungsprofile in OECD Demokratie*, pp. 321–54. Opladen, Germany: Leske und Büdrich, 2003.

Diener, Ed, and Carol Diener. "Most People Are Happy." *Psychological Science* 7, no. 3 (1996): 181–85.

Diener, Ed, Marissa Diener, and Carol Diener. "Factors Predicting the Subjective Well-Being of Nations." *Journal of Personality and Social Psychology* 69, no. 5 (1995): 851–64.

Diener, Ed, and Richard E. Lucas. "Personality and Subjective Well-Being." In Daniel Kahneman, Ed Diener, and Norbert Schwarz, eds. *Well-Being: The Foundation of*

Bibliography

Hedonic Psychology, pp. 213–29. New York: Russell Sage Foundation, 1999.

Diener, Ed, and Eunkook M. Suh. "Measuring Subjective Well-Being to Compare the Quality of Life of Cultures." In Diener and Suh, eds. *Culture and Subjective Well-Being*, pp. 3–13. Cambridge, MA and London: MIT Press, 2000.

Diener, Robert Biswas, Joar Vittersø, and Ed Diener. "Most People Are Pretty Happy, but There Is Cultural Variation: The Inughuit, the Amish, and the Maasai." *Journal of Happiness Studies* 6, no. 3 (2005): 205–26.

Dore, Ronald P. *Education in Tokugawa Japan*. Berkeley: University of California Press, 1965.

Dynan, Karen E., Douglas W. Elmendorf, and Daniel E. Sichel. "The Evolution of Household Income Volatility." *Finance and Economics Discussion Series* No. 61 (2007). Washington, DC: Federal Reserve Board.

England, Robert Stowe. *The Macroeconomic Impact of Global Aging*. Washington, D.C.: Center for Strategic and International Studies, 2002.

Floud, Roderick, and Donald McCloskey, eds. *The Economic History of Britain since 1700*. 2nd edition. New York: Cambridge University Press, 1994.

Food and Agricultural Organization. "FAO Food Price Index." 2008. http://www.fao.org/worldfoodsituation/FoodPriceIndex/en/.

Freedom House. *Freedom in the World*. 2008. http://www.freedomhouse.org.

Frey, Bruno S. *Happiness: A Revolution in Economics*. Cambridge, MA: MIT Press, 2008.

Frey, Bruno S., and Alois Stutzer. "Happiness, Economy and Institutions." *Economic Journal* 110, no. 466 (2000): 918–38.

Bibliography

Happiness and Economics: How the Economy and Institutions Affect Well-Being. Princeton, NJ: Princeton University Press, 2002.

Friedman, Milton. *Capitalism and Freedom*. Chicago: University of Chicago Press, 1962.

Germany, Statistisches Bundesamt. *Statistisches Jahrbuch 2005 für die Bundesrepublik Deutschlands*. Wiesbaden: Statistisches Bundesamt, 2005.

Glaeser, Edward L., and Andrei Shleifer. "Legal Origins." *Quarterly Journal of Economics* 117, no. 4 (2002): 1193–1229.

Golden, Miriam A., Michael Wallerstein, and Peter Lange. "Postwar Trade-Union Organization and Industrial Relations in Twelve Countries." In Herbert Kitschelt, Peter Lange, Gary Marks, and John D. Stephens, eds. *Continuity and Change in Contemporary Capitalism*, pp. 194–230. New York: Cambridge University Press, 1999.

Goody, Jack. *Capitalism and Modernity: The Great Debate*. Malden, MA: Polity Press, 2004.

Gosselin, Peter. *High Wire: The Precarious Financial Lives of American Families*. New York: Basic Books, 2008.

Grassby, Richard. *The Idea of Capitalism before the Industrial Revolution*. Lanham, MD: Rowman & Littlefield, 1999.

Greif, Avner. "Coercion and Exchange: How Did Markets Evolve?" 2008. http://ssrn.com/abstract=1304204.

Gwartney, James and Robert Lawson. *Various Years. Economic Freedom of the World* http://www.freetheworld.com/data-sets_efw.html.

Habib, Irfan. "Usury in Medieval India." *Comparative Studies in Society and History* 6, no. 4 (July 1964): 393–419.

Hall, John A. "States and Societies: The Miracle in Comparative Perspective." In Jean Baechler, John A. Hall, and Michael Mann, eds., 1988, pp. 20–39.

Bibliography

Hall, Peter A . and David Soskice, eds. *Varieties of Capitalism: The Institutional Foundations of Comparative Advantage*. New York: Oxford University Press, 2001.

Hallam, H. E. "The Medieval Social Picture." In Eugene Kamenka, Eugene and R. S. Neale, eds. *Feudalism, Capitalism and Beyond*, pp. 29–64. Canberra: Australian National University Press, 1973.

Heckscher, Eli F. *An Economic History of Sweden*. Translated by Gören Ohlin. Cambridge, MA: Harvard Unversity Press, 1963.

Helliwell, John. "How's Life? Combining Individual and National Variables to Explain Subjective Well-Being." *National Bureau of Economic Research Working Paper* No. 9065. Cambridge, MA: NBER, 2002.

Helliwell, John, and Haifang Huang. "How's Your Government? International Evidence Linking Good Government and Well-Being." *National Bureau of Economic Research Working Paper* No. 11988 (2006). Cambridge, MA: NBER

Heritage Foundation. *Index of Economic Freedom*. 2008 http://www.heritage.org/Index.

Hirschman, Albert O. *The Passions and the Interests: Political Arguments for Capitalism before Its Triumph*. Princeton, NJ: Princeton University Press, 1977.

Hofstede, Geert. *Culture's Consequences: Comparing Values, Behaviors, Organizations, and Organizations across Nations*. 2nd edition. Thousand Oaks, CA: Sage Publications, 2001.

Homer, Sidney. *A History of Interest Rates*. 2nd edition. New Brunswick, NJ: Rutgers University Press, 1977.

Homer, Sidney, and Richard Sylla. *A History of Interest Rates*. 3rd edition. New Brunswick, NJ: Rutgers University Press, 1996.

A History of Interest Rates. 4th edition. New Brunswick, NJ: Rutgers University Press, 2005.

Bibliography

Huang, Ray. *Taxation and Governmental Finance in Sixteenth-Century Ming China*. New York: Cambridge University Press, 1974.

Inglehart, Ronald, Miguel Basáñez, Jaime Díez-Medrano, Loek Halman, and Ruud Luijkx. *Human Beliefs and Values: A Cross-Cultural Sourcebook Based on the 1999–2002 Values Surveys*. Mexico City: Siglo XXI Editores, 2004.

Inglehart, Ronald, Miquel Basáñez, and Alejandro Moreno. *Human Values and Beliefs*. Ann Arbor, MI: University of Michigan Press, 1998.

International Labour Office. *Yearbook of Labour Statistics*. Published annually. Geneva: ILO.

Jacob, Margaret C. *Scientific Culture and the Making of the Industrial West*. New York: Oxford University Press, 1997.

Jefferson, Philip, and Frederic L. Pryor. "Dynamics of U.S. Factor Income Shares," *Journal of Income Distribution* 19, no. 1 (March 2010).

John Templeton Foundation, ed. *Does the Free Market Corrode Moral Character?* West Conshohocken, PA: Templeton, 2008.

Jones, Eric L. *The European Miracle: Environments, Economies, and Geopolitics in the History of Europe and Asia*. New York: Cambridge University Press, 1981.

Jones, Eric L., and Stuart J. Woolf. "The Historical Role of Agrarian Change in Economic Development." In Jones and Woolf, eds. *Agrarian Change and Economic Development*, pp. 10–23. London: Methuen & Co., 1969.

Kaufmann, Daniel, Aart Kraay, and Massimo Mastruzzi. 2005. "Government Matters IV: Aggregate and Individual Governance Indicators, 1996–2004." *World Bank Policy Research Working Paper Series* No. 3630.

Bibliography

"Governance Matters VI: Aggregate and Individual Governance Indicators." *World Bank Policy Research Working Paper Series* 4280. 2007. http://www.worldbank.org.

Keynes, John Maynard. *The General Theory of Employment, Interest, and Money.* New York: Harcourt, Brace, 1936.

Kroeber, Albert L., and Clyde Kluckholm. "Culture: A Critical Review of Concepts and Definitions." *Papers of the Peabody Museum of American Archeology and Ethnology* no. 47. Cambridge, MA: Peabody Museum, 1952.

Kuran, Timur. *The Long Divergence: How Islamic Law Held Back the Middle East.* Princeton, NJ: Princeton University Press, 2010.

Kurth, James. "A Tale of Four Countries: Parallel Politics in Southern Europe, 1815–1990." In James Kurth and James Petras, eds., pp. 27–66. *Mediterranean Paradoxes: Politics and Social Structure in Southern Europe.* Providence, RI: Berg, 1993.

Ladurie, Emmanuel Le Roy. *The Peasants of Languedoc.* Translated by John Day. Urbana: University of Illinois Press, 1974.

Lindert, Peter H. *Growing Public: Social Spending and Economic Growth since the Eighteenth Century.* New York: Cambridge University Press, 2004.

"Life Expectancy Data," 2008. http://gpih.ucdavis.edu/Evidence.htm.

Luxembourg Income Study. "Key Figures." 2008. http://www.lisproject.org/keyfigures.htm.

Macfarlane, Alan. *The Origins of English Individualism.* New York: Cambridge University Press, 1979.

Maddison, Angus. "A Comparison of Levels of GDP Per Capita in Developed and Developing Countries, 1700–1980." *Journal of Economic History* 43, no. 1 (March 1983): 27–41.

"Measuring European Growth: The Core and the Periphery." In Erik Aerts and N. Valério, eds. *Proceedings of the Tenth International Economic History Congress Leuven*, pp. 82–118. Belgium: Leuven University Press, 1990.

The World Economy: Historical Statistics. Paris: OECD, 2003.

Mann, Michael. "European Development: Approaching a Historical Explanation." pp. 1–6 in Baechler, Hall, and Mann, eds., 1988.

Marshall, Monty G., and Keith Jaggers. *Polity IV Project: Political Regime Characteristics and Transitions, 1800–2004.* 2005. http://www.cidem.umd.edu/polity.

Maxwell, Bruce A., Frederic L. Pryor, and Casey Smith. "Cluster Analysis in Cross-Cultural Research," *World Cultures* 13, no. 1 (2002): 22–39.

Mielants, Eric H. *The Origins of Capitalism and the Rise of the West.* Philadelphia: Temple University Press, 2007.

Minsky, Hyman. *Stabilizing an Unstable Economy.* New York: McGraw Hill, 2008.

Miringoff, Marque-Luisa, and Sandra Opdycke. *America's Social Health.* Armonk, NY: M. E. Sharpe, 2008.

Mokyr, Joel. *The Gifts of Athena: Historical Origins of the Knowledge Economy.* Princeton, NJ: Princeton University Press, 2002.

Moosvi, Shireen. *People, Taxation, and Trade in Mughal India.* New York: Oxford University Press, 2008.

Needham, Joseph. *The Grand Titration: Science and Society in East and West.* London: Allen & Unwin, 1969.

Nicoletti, Giuseppe, and Frederic L. Pryor. "Subjective and Objective Measures of the Extent of Government Regulation," *Journal of Economic Behavior and Organization* 59, no. 3 (1995): 433–449. http://papers.ssrn.com/sol3/papers.cfm?abstract_id=285494.

Nicoletti, Giuseppe, Stefano Scarpetta, and Olivier Boylaud. "Summary Indicators of Product Market Regulation with an Extension to Employment Protection Legislation." *OECD Economics Department Working Papers* No. 237. Paris: OECD, 1999.

North, Douglass C. *Structure and Change in Economic History*. New York: Norton & Co., 1981.

"Economic Performance through Time." In Carl K. Eicher and John M. Staatz, eds. *International Agricultural Development*. 3rd edition, pp. 78–90. Baltimore, MD: Johns Hopkins University Press, 1998.

North, Douglass C., and Robert Paul Thomas. *The Rise of the Western World: A New Economic History*. Cambridge: Cambridge University Press, 1973.

Nurullah, Syed, and J. P. Naik. *A Student's History of Education in India, 1800–1965*. 5th rev. ed. Bombay: Macmillan, 1964.

Organization of Economic Cooperation and Development. *OECD Health Data 2000*. CD ROM. Paris: OECD, 2000.

Labour Force Statistics, 1983–2003. Paris: OECD, 2004.

OECD Health Data 2007. CD ROM. Paris: OECD, 2007.

Growing Unequal? Income Distribution and Poverty in OECD Countries. Paris: OECD, 2008.

Ouweenel, P., and Ruut Veenhoven. "Cross-National Differences in Happiness: Cultural Bias or Societal Quality?" In Nico Bleichrodt and Pieter J. D. Drenth, eds. *Contempory Issues in Cross-Cultural Psychology*, pp. 168–84. Amsterdam: Svets and Zeitlinger, 1991.

Passow, Richard. *"Kapitalismus": Eine begrifflich-terminologische Studie*. Jena, Germany: Gustav Fischer, 1927.

Patrick, Hugh T. "Japan: 1868–1914." In Rondo Cameron, et al. eds. *Banking in the Early Stages of Industrialization*, pp. 239–89. New York: Oxford University Press, 1967.

Peacock, Alan T., and Jack Wiseman. *The Growth of Public Expenditures in the United Kingdom*. Princeton, NJ: Princeton University Press, 1961.

Bibliography

Perlin, Frank. "Financial Institutions and Business Practices Across the Euro-Asian Interface: Comparative and Structural Considerations, 1500–1900." In Hans Pohl, ed. *The European Discovery of the World and Its Economic Effects on Pre-Industrial Society, 1500–1900*, pp. 257–304. Stuttgart: Steiner Verlag, 1990.

Persson, Torsten, and Guido Tabellini. *The Economic Effects of Constitutions*. Cambridge, MA: MIT Press, 2003.

Pomeranz, Kenneth. *The Making of a Hinterland: State, Society, and Economy in Inland North China*. Berkeley: University of California Press, 1993.

    The Great Divergence. Princeton, NJ: Princeton University Press, 2000.

    "Land Markets in Late Imperial and Republican China," *Continuity and Change* 23, no. 1(2008): 101–150.

Pontusson, Jonas. *Inequality and Prosperity: Social Europe vs. Liberal America*. Ithaca: Cornell University Press, 2005.

Posner, Richard A. *A Failure of Capitalism: The Crisis of '08 and the Descent into Depression*. Cambridge, MA: Harvard University Press, 2009.

Pryor, Frederic L. "The Extent and Pattern of Public Ownership in Developed Economies," *Weltwirtschaftliches Archiv* 102, no. 1 (1970): 159–188.

    "An International Comparison of Concentration Ratios," *Review of Economics and Statistics* 54, no. 2 (1972): 130–40.

    The Origins of the Economy: A Comparative Study of Distribution in Primitive and Peasant Economies. New York: Academic Press, 1977.

    "The Origins of Money," *Journal of Money, Credit, and Banking* 9, no. 3 (August 1977): 391–409.

    "Climatic Fluctuations as a Cause of Differential Economic Growth of the Orient and Occident: A Comment." *Journal*

Bibliography

of Economic History 45, no. 3 (September 1985): 667–675, 683.

"Growth and Fluctuations of Production in O.E.C.D. and East European Nations," *World Politics* 37, no. 2 (January 1095): 204–38.

"Corporatism as an Economic System." *Journal of Comparative Economics* 12, no. 3 (September 1988): 317–44.

"The Performance of Agricultural Production in Marxist and Non-Marxist Nations," *Comparative Economic Studies* 33, no. 3 (1991): 95–127.

The Future of U.S. Capitalism. New York: Cambridge University Press, 2002.

"Demographic Effects on Personal Saving in the Future." *Southern Economic Journal* 69, no. 3 (January 2003): 541–60.

"Economic Systems of Foragers." *Cross-Cultural Research* 37, no. 4 (November 2003): 393–427.

Economic Systems of Foraging, Agricultural, and Industrial Societies. New York: Cambridge University Press, 2005.

Economic Systems of Foraging, Agricultural, and Industrial Societies. 2005. Appendices 7–1 and 7–2 http://www.swarthmore.edu/SocSci/Economics/fpryor1.

"National Values and Economic Growth," *American Journal of Economics and Sociology,* 64, no. 2 (April 2005): 451–85

"Rethinking Economic Systems: A Study of Agricultural Societies." *Cross-Cultural Research* 39, no. 3 (August 2005): 252–93.

"Economic Systems of Developing Nations," *Comparative Economic Studies* 48, no. 1 (March 2006): 77–98.

"Cultural and Economic Systems." *American Journal of Economics and Sociology* 66, no. 4 (October 2007): 817–55.

Bibliography

"Systems as Causal Forces." *Journal of Economic Behavior and Organization* 67, no. 3 (September 2008): 545–59.

"Transaction Costs on a National Level: Causes and Consequences." *Journal of Institutional and Theoretical Economics* 164, no. 4 (December 2008): 676–95.

"Capitalism and Freedom?" *Economic Systems* 34, no. 2: 91–104.

"The Political Economy of a Semi-Industrialized Theocratic State: The Islamic Republic of Iran." In Ronald Wintrobe and Mario Ferroro, eds. *The Political Economy of Theocracy.* New York: Palgrave/Macmillan, 2009.

Ratnovski, Lev, and Rocco Huang. "Why Are Canadian Banks More Resilient?" *IMF Working Paper Working Paper/09/152* (2009).

Rawski, Evelyn Sakakida. *Education and Popular Literacy in Ch'ing China.* Ann Arbor, MI: University of Michigan Press, 1979.

"Functional Literacy in Nineteenth-Century China." In Daniel P. Resnick, ed. *Literacy in Historical Perspective*, pp. 85–105. Washington, DC: Library of Congress, 1983.

Rissanen, Jorma. *Stochastic Complexity in Statistical Inquiry.* Singapore: World Scientific, 1989.

"Information, Complexity and the MDL Principle." In Lionello F. Punzo, ed. *Cycles, Growth and Structural Change: Theories and Empirical Evidence*, pp. 339–51. New York: Routledge, 2001.

Romesburg, H. Charles. *Cluster Analysis for Researchers.* Belmont CA: Lifelong Learning Publications, 1984.

Ross, Myron H. "Fluctuations in Economic Activity." *American Economic Review* 55, no. 1 (March 1965): 158–61.

Samuelsson, Kurt. *Religion and Economic Action; A Critique of Max Weber.* Translated by E. Geoffrey French. New York: Harper & Row, 1964.

Bibliography

Sanderson, Michael. "Literacy and Social Mobility in the Industrial Revolution in England." *Past and Present* 56 (August 1972): 75–104.

Schneider, Friedrich, and Dominik Enste. *The Shadow Economy: An International Survey.* New York: Cambridge University Press, 2000.

Shimbo, Hiroshi, and Osamu Saitô. "The Economy on the Eve of Industrialization." In Akira Hayami, Osamu Saitô, and Ronald P. Toby, eds. *The Economic History of Japan: 1600–1990.* Vol. 1. pp. 337–68. New York: Oxford University Press, 2004.

Smil, Vaclav. 1994. *Energy in World History.* Boulder, CO: Westview.

Smith, Thomas C. *The Agrarian Origins of Modern Japan.* Stanford, CA: Stanford University Press, 1959.

Sobel, Russell S., and Christopher J. Coyne. "Cointegrating Institutions: The Time-Series Properties of Country Institutional Measures," *Journal of Law and Economics,* forthcoming.

Stenkula, Mikael. 2006. "The European Size Distribution of Firms and Employment." Research Institute of Industrial Economics, IFN Working Paper No. 683 (2006). Stockholm: RIIE.

Stevenson, Betsey, and Justin Wolfers. "Economic Growth and Subjective Well-Being: Reassessing the Easterlin Paradox." 2008. http://bpp.wharton.upenn.edu/betseys/papers/happiness.pdf.

Stolper, Wolfgang. *The Structure of the East German Economy.* Cambridge, MA: Harvard University Press, 1960.

Sugden, Robert. "Normative Expectations: The Simultaneous Evolution of Institutions and Norms." In Avner Ben-Nur and Louis Putterman, eds. *Economics, Values, and Organizations,* pp. 73–100. New York: Cambridge University Press, 1998.

Bibliography

Takekoshi, Yosoburo. 1930. *The Economic Aspects of the History of the Civilization of Japan.* New York: Macmillan.

Tashiro, Kazui. "Foreign Trade in the Tokugawa Period – Particularly with Korea." In Akira Hayami, Osamu Saitô, and Ronald P. Toby, eds. *Emergence of Economic Society in Japan 1600–1859.* Vol. 1, pp. 105–18. New York: Oxford University Press, 2003.

Thackeray, William Makepeace. *The Newcomes: Memoirs of a Most Respectable Family.* New York: Harper & Bros., 1855 (also Ann Arbor, MI: University of Michigan Press, 1996).

Thesaurus Linguae Latinae. 1906–12. Leipzig: Teubner.

Toninelli, Piet Angelo. *The Rise and Fall of State-Owned Enterprise in the Western World.* New York: Cambridge University Press, 2000.

Tsai, Kellee S. *Capitalism without Democracy: The Private Sector in Contemporary China.* Ithaca, NY: Cornell University Press, 2007.

UK Data Archive . *European Values Survey: User Notes.* 2005. http://www.data-archiv.ac.uk.

United Nations. *Demographic Yearbook,* published annually. New York: United Nations.

United Nations. *World Population Prospects: The 2002 Revision.* Vol. 1. New York: United Nations, 2003.

United Nations Development Programme. *Human Development Report 1998.* New York: Oxford University Press, 1998.

United Nations Framework Convention on Climate Change (UNFCCC). *GHC Data from UNFCCC,* 2008. http://unfccc.int/ghg_data/ghg_data_unfccc/items/4146.php.

U.S. Bureau of the Census. *Statistics of U.S. Businesses.* 2008. http://www.census.gov/csd/susb.

Veenhoven, Rutt. "Quality-of-Life in Individualistic Societies: A Comparison in 43 Nations in the Early 1990's." *Social Indicators Research* 48, no. 2 (1999): 157–86.

Bibliography

"Freedom and Happiness: A Comparative Study in Forty-Four Nations in the Early 1990s." 2000, pp. 257–88. In Diener and Suh.

"Comparability of Happiness across Nations." 2008. http://www2.cur.nl/fsw/research/veenhoven/Pub2000s/2008f-full.pdf.

World Database of Happiness. 2008. http://www.worlddatabaseofhappiness.eur.nl.

Veenhoven, Rutt, et al. *World Database of Happiness: Correlates of Happiness: 7838 Findings from 603 Studies in 69 Nations.*1994. http://www.worlddatabaseofhappiness.edu.nl.

Veenhoven, Ruut, and Wim Kalmijn. "Inequality-Adjusted Happiness in Nations: Egalitarianism and Utilitarianism Married Together in a New Index of Societal Performance." *Journal of Happiness Studies* 6, no. 4 (2005): 421–55.

Visser, Jelle. "Union Membership Statistics in 24 Countries." *Monthly Labor Review* 129, no. 1 (January 2006), 38–49.

Voigt, Stefan and Sang-Min Park. "Values and Norms Matter: On the Basic Determinants of Long-Run Economic Development." 2008. http://ssrn.com/abstract=1165343.

Weber, Max. *The Protestant Ethic and the Spirit of Capitalism.* Translated by Talcott Parsons. New York: Routledge, 1930 [1905].

The Theory of Social and Economic Organization. Translated by A. M. Henderson and Talcott Parsons, New York: Oxford University Press, 1947 [1922].

Wikipedia. "Unitary State." 2008. http://en.wikipedia.org/wiki/Unitary_state.

Wood, Ellen Meiksins. *The Origins of Capitalism: A Longer View.* New York: Verso, 2002.

World Bank. *World Development Indicators.* 2008. http://www.worldbank.org.

Bibliography

World Resources Institute. 2008. http://earthtrends.wri.org/ searchable_db/index.php?theme=3.

Wrigley, Edgar Anthony. 2000. "The Divergence of England: The Growth of the English Economy in the Seventeenth and Eighteenth Centuries." *Transactions of the Royal Historical Society.* 6th series, 10 (2008): 117–41.

Zweynert, Joachim, and Nils Goldschmidt. "The Two Transitions in Central and Eastern Europe as Processes of Institutional Transplantation." *Journal of Economic Issues* 40, no. 4 (2006): 895–918.

Index

Adelman, Irma, 11, 12, 23, 148, 150
Akerlof, George A., 173
Akira Hayami, 61
Allen, Robert, 28
Amable, Bruno, 89
Angus Maddison, 27
animal spirits, 172
appendices, 7
Aristotle, 156, 183
Aston, Trevor Henry, 41
Australia, 24, 86, 87, 106, 116, 158, 191, 207
Austria, 24, 25, 86, 116, 133, 159, 191, 207
Austro-Hungary, 50

Bäckman, Olof, 163
Bacon, Francis, 30
Bairoch, Paul, 25, 28, 40
Balkans, 25
Barbera, Robert J., 173
Barth, Erling, 145
Belgium, 24, 27, 50, 86, 116, 159, 191, 207, 256

Berman, Harold, 34
Bernhardt, Kathryn, 55
Biswas, Robert, 189
Bolivia, 150
Bowles, Samuel, 139
Braudel, Fernand, 44
Brenner, Robert, 41
Brickman, Philip, 204

Canada, 24, 25, 86, 87, 106, 116, 158, 177, 191, 207
capital/labor relations, 219
capitalism, 7–8
    change, 205
    characteristics, 90
    classification, 76
    country classification, 86
    definition, 7
    economic development, 23
    education, 48
    environment, 67
    government, 52
    growth and fluctuations, 207
    institutions, 33

Index

capitalism (*cont.*)
  level of development, 24
  level of economic development, 86
  markets, 35
  measurement, 18
  origins, 20
  political centralization, 54
  prerequisites, 10, 13, 14
  private property, 43
  Protestantism, 61
  social factors, 61
  spirit, 63
  spirit of, 7
  technology, 30
  threshhold, 23
  threshhold year, 24, 53
  values, 63
  varieties, 74
causation
  lineal, 152
  systemic, 152, 161
China, 25, 27, 37, 46, 50
Cipolla, Carlo M., 6, 48, 50
cluster analysis, 76, 77
  diagram, 78
  optimal number, 81
Coates, Dan, 204
commerce, 60
consumer debt, 237
Corning, Peter, 156
Costa Rica, 150
cultural systems, 115
  causal factors, 127, 130
  characteristics, 117, 118
  country composition, 116, 158
  stability, 127
culture
  definition, 113

democracy, 16
demography, 210
Denmark, 24, 25, 30, 50, 86, 116, 158, 191, 207
Diener, Carol, 189
Diener, Ed, 188, 189
Diener, Robert, 189
Dore, Ronald, 50

East European countries, 133
economic development
  estimation, 11
  influence, 23
economic development level, 138
economic freedom
  relation to political freedom, 147
economic growth, 217
economic system
  Anglo-Saxon, 87, 89
  change, 221
  characteristics, 90
  definition, 8
  happiness, 203
  impact, 146
  level of development, 106
  Nordic, 87, 89
  political factors, 106
  South European, 87, 89
  West European, 87, 89
economic systems
  causal factors, 127, 130
  converging, diverging, 229
  country composition, 116, 158
  location, 104
  parallel country changes, 225
  parallel institutional changes, 222
  performance, 146

Index

education
  literacy, 48
England, 24, 46
England/Wales, 50
Ethiopia, 150

feudalism, 102
financial crisis, 176
financial sector, 235
Finland, 86, 103, 105, 116, 133, 158,
  159, 191, 207
food prices, 215
foreign trade, 212
France, 24, 38, 46, 50, 56, 59, 86,
  87, 94, 105, 106, 116, 159, 169,
  191, 207, 250
Frey, Bruno S., 185, 189
Friedman, Milton, 147, 148, 151

Germany, 24, 46, 86, 112, 116, 131,
  132, 133, 134, 135, 136, 138,
  139, 144, 157, 159, 191, 207,
  239, 257
Germany, East, 131
Germany, West, 116, 131, 157, 159
Glaeser, Edward L., 181
globalization, 211, 239
  transmission of shocks, 213
Goldschmidt, Nils, 136, 137
Goody, Jack, 48, 62
government
  attitudes toward commerce, 57
  role, 52
  size of, 238
governmental policy, 238
Grassby, Richard, 76
Greece, 25, 86, 105, 116, 159, 163,
  164, 191, 195, 207

Greenspan, Alan, 177
Greif, Avner, 45
Guatemala, 150

Hall, John A., 48, 52, 54
Hall, Peter A., 88
Hallam, H.E., 62
happiness, 184
  causes of, 185, 197
  components, 199
  determinants, 196
  measurement, 187
  measures, 191
Heckscher, Eli, 102, 103
Helliwell, John, 185
Hirschman, Albert O., 17, 63, 141
housing bubble, 175
Huang, Haifang, 185
Huang, Ray, 58
Huang, Philip C.C., 55

India, 27, 46, 50
Inglehart, Ronald, 64, 114, 128, 243
institution
  definition, 74
institutional approach, 2
institutional change, 206
  speed, 231
institutions, change, 210
interest rate, 45
  See also private property
interest rates, 46
Ireland, 86, 87, 116, 158, 191, 207
Italy, 24, 38, 46, 49, 50, 51, 86, 107,
  108, 109, 116, 159, 191, 207

Jacob, Margaret C., 47
Jaggers, Keith, 53, 148, 149, 150

Index

Janoff-Bulman, Janoff, 204
Japan, 20, 25, 27, 30, 33, 36, 37, 38,
    44, 46, 47, 50, 51, 54, 60, 62,
    67, 68, 70, 71, 72, 79, 86, 87,
    104, 105, 108, 109, 116, 118,
    125, 141, 159, 163, 164, 191,
    207, 261, 262
John Templeton Foundation, 139

Kalmijn, Wim, 190, 191, 263
Keynes, John Maynard, 172
Kluckholm, Clyde, 113
Korea, 150
Korea, North and South, 132
Korea, South, 150
Kroeber, Albert L., 113
Kuran, Timur, 20, 71
Kurth, James, 107

labor
    markets, 220
    sector, 241
Ladurie, Emannuel Le Roy, 67
Levy-Leboyer, Maurice, 28
Liberia, 150
life expectancy, 29
Lindert Peter, 30
literacy, 48
literacy rates, 50
Lucas, Richard E., 189

Maastricht agreement, 84
Macfarlane, Alan, 102
Maddison, Angus, 13, 25, 26, 27,
    29, 86, 106, 150, 234
Mann, Michael, 31, 32
market
    government sector, 92
    labor market, 91

place, 38
product market, 90
production and business, 92
marketization, 150
Marshal, Monty, 53
Marshall, Monty, 53, 148, 149,
    150, 151
Marx, Karl, 16, 141
Maxwell, Bruce A., 78
Mexico, 25
Mielants, Eric H., 20, 56, 57, 62, 141
minimum description length
    (MDL), 81
Minsky, Hyman, 173
Miringoff, Marque-Louisa, 170
Moene, Karl O., 145
Mokyr, Joel, 48
Morris, Cynthia Taft, 11, 12, 23,
    148, 150

Naik, J.P., 50
natural resources, 214
Needham, Joseph, 52, 58, 59
Netherland, 191
Netherlands, 12, 24, 26, 46, 50, 86,
    116, 159
New Zealand, 24, 86, 87, 106, 116,
    158, 169, 191, 207
North, Douglas C., 43, 67, 74
Norway, 24, 25, 86, 105, 116, 158,
    176, 177, 191, 207
Nurullah, Syed, 50

O'Brien, Patrick, 44
Opdycke, Sandra, 170
Orange Free State, 150
organizations
    definition, 74
Ouweenel, P., 189

Index

Park, San-Min, 67
Patrick, Hugh, 37
Peacock, Alan T., 142
performance systems
  characteristics, 162
  country composition, 158, 160
  definition, 157
Perlin, Frank, 37
Peru, 150
Philpin, C.H.E., 41
Polanyi, Karl, 36
political centralization, 53
political freedom
  measurement, 149
  relation to capitalism, 147
Pomeranz, Kenneth, 28, 30, 31, 37,
  67, 70, 72
Pontusson, Jonas, 89
Pope Gregory, 34
Portugal, 25, 60, 86, 107, 116, 159,
  191, 207
Posner, Richard, 174
property. See also capitalism
Prussia, 50
Pryor, iv, xi, 49, 114, 169
Pryor, Frederic L., 11, 15, 35, 48,
  49, 78, 82, 88, 94, 107, 114,
  132, 138, 148, 151, 170, 209,
  211, 212, 214, 217, 219, 226,
  227, 229, 242

Rawski, Evelyn Sakakida, 48, 49, 50
Rissanen, Jorma, 80
Romesburg, H. Charles, 78
Russia, 25, 46, 50, 133, 206

Samuelsson, Kurt, 62
Sanderson, Michael, 48, 49
savings rate, 216

Scotland, 50
Serbia, 150
Shiller, Robert J., 173
Shleifer, Andrei, 181
Smil, Vaclav, 29, 31
Smith, Casey, 78
Smith, Thomas C., 25
social classes, 16
Soskice, David, 88
Spain, 24, 49, 50, 51, 60, 86, 107,
  116, 159, 191, 207
stage theories, 11
Stevenson, Betsey, 190
Stolper, Wolfgang, 131
Stutzer, Alois, 185, 189
Sugden, Robert, 130
Suh, Eunkook M., 188
Sweden, 24, 25, 30, 46, 50, 86, 103,
  104, 116, 158, 177, 191, 195,
  207, 253
Switzerland, 24, 50, 86, 87, 94, 104,
  106, 116, 117, 158, 159, 163,
  176, 191, 207
systemic causation, 177

Tashiro, Kazui, 61
Thatcher, Margaret, 206, 228
Thomas, Robert Paul, 43, 67
trade. See capitalism, markets
transaction costs, 170

unemployment, 125
United Kingdom, 27, 86, 116, 158,
  191, 206, 207, 227
  economic system. See England
United States, 24, 46, 50, 86, 116,
  158, 191, 207
  founder effects, 143
urbanization, 24, 38

Index

values. *See* capitalism, values
Veenhoven, Ruut, 188, 189,
   190, 191, 192
Vitters, Joar, 189
Voigt, Stefan, 67
volatility
  macroeconomic, 217
  microeconomic, 218

Weber, Max, 17, 61, 101,
   141
Wiseman, Jack, 142
Wolfers, Justin, 190
Wood, Evelyn, 59
Wrigley, E.A., 69

Zweynert, Joachim, 136, 137

Printed in the United States
by Baker & Taylor Publisher Services